£12·50

(7)

D1101354

# THE TRAGEDY OF HMS DASHER

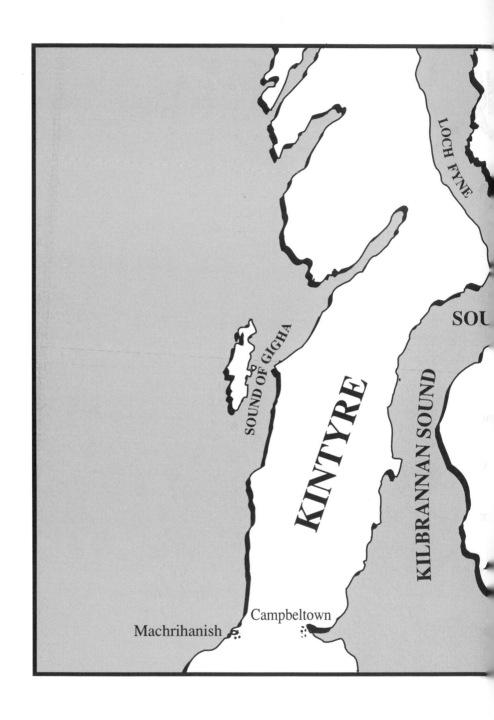

Dasher *lies at 55° 37.73" North, 05° 00.92" West*
*The wreck is a designated war grave*

# THE TRAGEDY OF HMS *DASHER*

## JOHN STEELE

© John Steele

First Published 1995
Argyll Publishing
Glendaruel
Argyll PA22 3AE

The author has asserted his moral rights.

**British Library Cataloguing-in-Publication Data.
A catalogue record for this book is available from
the British Library.**

ISBN 1 874640 41 6

*Typeset & Origination*
Cordfall Ltd, Glasgow

*Printing*
Bookcraft (Bath) Ltd.

This book is dedicated
to the officers and men who
perished when HMS *Dasher*
sank on 27th March 1943.

*"We will remember them"*

# Acknowledgements

For their help in compiling this memorial book I wish to record my thanks to the following.

The survivors who shared their memories;
the bereaved families who shared painful memories and allowed me to use precious photographs;
John Brown from Fairlie who advised me on nautical terminology;
Judith Davenport;
T McKay MBE, Chairman, Royal Naval Assoc, Scottish Branch;
the Naval Historical Branch, London;
HM Coastguard, Greenock;
Royal National Lifeboat Institution;
Martin Wallace, formerly of the *Ardrossan & Saltcoats Herald*;
Ardrossan Library;
Bill Haggerty of Ayr for legal advice;
Cunningham District Council for their support;
the Wrecks Officer, Hydrographic Office, Taunton;
Denise McLellan MA (HONS);
Barbara Kay of Ayr;

the Scottish Maritime Museum, Irvine;
Captain Archie Murchie;
Commander R Kirkwood, Royal Navy;
Horst Bredow, U-Boot Archives, Cuxhaven, Germany;
David Hendry, Largs;
Ministry of Defence, Secretariat (Naval Staff), London;
Commonwealth War Graves Commisssion, Maidenhead;
and Noreen for her patience, assistance and support.

John Steele
Ardrossan March 1995

# CONTENTS

# ILLUSTRATIONS

# FOREWORD

Wars throw up innumerable tragedies, which indelibly mark the lives of those who witness or survive them. The loss of HMS *Dasher* cost 379 lives, but until now has remained one of the little-told stories of the Second World War.

In home waters it was second only to the loss of the *Royal Oak* at Scapa Flow in the grim league table of British naval disasters during that conflict. Yet it has remained as the merest footnote in naval history—the mass sacrifice by men of the Royal Navy which many have preferred not to talk about.

Perhaps one of the reasons for this lies in the fact HMS *Dasher* and 379 lives were not lost through enemy action.

For many years, the understandable secrecy which had shrouded wartime events was sustained. There have been no previous books written about the *Dasher*, and even its name is familiar only to the most devoted students of military history.

However for thousands of individuals the tragedy has lived on in their minds and memories. They include the small number of survivors—a few of whom have returned regularly to the scene—and the bereaved, who lost their loved ones in these unexplained and incomprehensible circumstances.

The story of HMS *Dasher* is also familiar to many on the Clyde coast, particularly in Ardrossan and on the island of Arran. It was from these communities that the rescue efforts and care for survivors came, and it was on these shores that the wreckage washed up in the months that followed the explosion and sinking. In 1993, a memorial to those lost on HMS *Dasher* was finally created in Ardrossan.

John Steele's *The Tragedy of* HMS *Dasher* ensures at last that a proper record of this sad episode is available for all time. His researches have produced a startling account of the sinking and the catastrophic circumstances that surrounded it. New eye-witness and survivor accounts, photographs never before published and even a sonar scan of the wreck on the sea bed all help to tell the story in graphic detail.

This impressively detailed and moving book is a fitting memorial to those who lost their lives. It is also enriched by the memories of those whose rights and needs were overlooked, first in the greater cause of the war effort and then by bureaucracy's preference to conceal. The bereaved never got to know officially how their loved ones died. Indeed such were the circumstances at the time that some of the contents of this book will be news even to some of those who lived through these events.

Fifty years on, John Steele's account is an important reminder— still highly relevant today—of the need for maritime safety never to be overlooked. As we survey the virtual extinction of the British Merchant Navy, we might also pause to wonder where the seafaring skills that Britain has relied on so heavily in the past would come from in the future, if ever a similar call arose.

Brian Wilson MP

CHAPTER 1

# 27th MARCH 1943
# DISASTER DAY

It was a sunny spring afternoon and offshore in the River Clyde estuary between the Ayrshire town of Ardrossan and the Isle of Arran a British aircraft carrier had been conducting deck landing practice. For most of the day the aircraft had continually flown off from, circled then landed back on board. HMS *Dasher* had a compliment of five hundred and twenty eight personnel.

Shortly after 4.30pm, the ship's master, Captain Boswell, announced over the tannoy that shore leave was being granted on arrival at the port of Greenock. The estimated time of arrival was 6.00pm and a signal was relayed from the aircraft carrier as to its intentions.

The off-duty crew, many of them preparing for an evening ashore, were below deck. Some were having a wash and a shave.

During the flying operations the duty Air Sea Rescue Launch circled the ship. It noted that in the immediate vicinity were the destroyer *La Capricieuse*, the radar training ship *Isle of Sark* and two coastal vessels, the *Lithium* and the *Cragsman*.

On completion of the deck landing practice the state of HMS *Dasher* was as follows. All aircraft except one had been struck down. In the hangar below decks were six Swordfish and two Sea Hurricanes. Two Swordfish at the time of the Captain's announcement were being refuelled.

HMS *Dasher*, like her sister ships of the same model, had been detailed to escort duty to protect the crucial North Atlantic corridor. With the presence of a carrier, planes could do constant reconnaissance to protect cargo fleets from the attentions of the pervasive and dangerous presence of German U-boats.

As a consequence an escort carrier like *Dasher* had an impressive compliment of men and a considerable quota of arms and equipment on board.

As well as the aircraft themselves, at this time in the afternoon, work had just been completed in the after depth charge stowage. Sixty eight depth charges were contained in the magazine. The stowage tanks contained seventy five thousand gallons of fuel and the aviation fuel tanks contained enough fuel for fifteen aircraft.

On the bridge, Lt Commander Lane was checking the charts. Suddenly the ship shuddered and an explosion was heard. Then another almighty explosion.

The officer of the watch was heard to say, "Crikey, look at that!" The Captain and the officers on the bridge looked in astonishment as they saw the lift between the aircraft deck and the hangar soaring high in the sky, perfectly horizontal. It reached a height of around sixty feet before plunging into the sea, port side.

Smoke and flames were rising from the aircraft lift shaft and the flight deck was buckled up to half the length of the hangar. To starboard there were bursts in the ship's side, out of which smoke and flames were visible.

The ship was settling by the stern. However the buoyancy of the hanger was resisting the pull at the stern. The aircraft carrier was beginning to groan and creak. Plates sprung as the bow fought a battle with the stern.

Immediately after the first explosion, every machine on the ship stopped. All lights went out and there were no ship's noises. Twenty

*Flying off* Dasher

*Fleet Air Arm personnel (with camera) prepare for landing on* Dasher

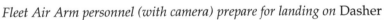

*Sea Hurricane with arrestor down, about to land on* Dasher *(February 1943)*

*Swordfish about to land on* Dasher

seconds later the lights came back on and immediately went out again. There was then no more power and the ship was in complete darkness. Fires had started in various parts of the ship and some of the crew progressed along passageways by the flickering light of the flames.

On the bridge Captain Boswell ordered Lt Commander Lane to find out what was happening. The Lt Commander made his way below deck where he encountered volumes of smoke and tongues of flame. He heard the sound of rushing water and the grinding of metal. On reaching the third deck, he found it to be under three feet of water. Quickly retracing his steps along the smoke-filled passageway, he checked the cabins and offices to make sure they were empty. On his return to the upper deck level he found that the water was already coming over it.

Below deck some of the crew were trying to prise open a buckled door. They were frantically using every conceivable tool they could lay their hands on. Suddenly the ship shuddered and the door straightened out sufficiently to allow the struggling seamen to open it.

The two dreadful explosions had resulted in the complete destruction of the Fleet Air Arm mess deck, a violent fire in the after end of the hangar, a serious fire in the engine room and rapid flooding of the ship. On the deck, Lt Commander Lane was trying to get the crew to swing out the lifeboats. However as the bow of the ship was all the while rising higher and higher out of the water, this was not so easy. It was now time to follow Captain Boswell's last order. Abandon Ship! Abandon Ship!

Lt Commander Nigel Bailey, Commanding Officer of 891 Squadron was in the squadron office immediately below the flight deck when the ship shuddered violently and the fearful explosion occurred. He made his way to the ready room to collect his Mae-West. On reaching the flight deck, he reported that the ship was well down by the stern and there were many fires burning. The hoses were being coupled up to fight the fires when Nigel Bailey saw one of his own Sea Hurricanes slithering out of control down the, by now, steeply angled flight deck, heading straight towards him. He quickly jumped out of its erratic path and watched the pilot-less plane topple unmajestically over the side into the Firth of Clyde. Then he heard the Abandon Ship! order and he himself jumped into the water.

At the time of the explosion, air mechanic William Macdonald was in his cabin looking in his kitbag for his shaving gear. He was blown through a hole which had appeared in the ship's side, and he landed in the water four hundred yards away. He was plucked from the water almost immediately by *Dasher*'s duty motor launch. He was still clutching his kitbag.

Sub Lt Ferrier was below deck when the lights went out. He had joined the carrier in New York and fortunately he was by this time very familiar with the layout of the passageways. Accompanied by Sub Lt Tetlow, he very quickly made his way on deck which was, by now, very steep. He took off his jacket and from a height of sixty feet above the water, jumped overboard. Plunging into the water, he went down very deep and it seemed such a long lung-bursting time before he resurfaced. He was not a good swimmer and as he struggled to stay afloat he realised that Sub Lt Tetlow was not to be seen. The ship was almost vertical and as he swam away as far as possible, he could hear those still on board screaming below deck as the carrier rose completely vertical and slid beneath the waves.

As the ship disappeared, Sub Lt Ferrier saw a biscuit tin floating quite near. He swam towards it and held on. At this point he realised that the ship's fuel tanks had been ruptured and he was surrounded by seventy five thousand gallons of black diesel. Suddenly there was a loud Whoosh! and the sea caught fire. The searing sea of flame entrapped many of his shipmates who were in the water and he could hear the screams and shouts. The Sub Lt could do nothing to help. As the screaming and shouting went on, he watched helplessly as his shipmates burned to death. Before long the screaming and shouting stopped.

A massive sea rescue operation was immediately set in motion. The two explosions on board the carrier, the ship sinking and the sea of flame resulted in the loss of a high number of the ship's personnel.

As one hundred and forty nine survivors were brought ashore at HMS *Fortitude* (the wartime name for Ardrossan harbour), they were

*HMS* Isle of Sark—*four miles north of* Dasher *at the time of the explosion*

subject to a further order. They had not to discuss what had happened, where it had happened, or any other circumstances whatsoever. They were allowed to contact their relatives, but only to inform them that they would "soon be home on leave".

A blanket of secrecy was imposed by the Royal Navy to ensure that the enemy did not find out the fate of the aircraft carrier. Such information was felt to have been of great value, especially to Admiral Doenitz who was at that time probably feeling a sense of satisfaction over recent results. Twenty Allied merchant ships totalling 141,000 tons had been sunk during the month of March 1943, all the work of thirty eight U-boats under his command. Because of the range and attack powers aircraft carriers gave Allied convoys, the movements of carriers were considered priceless intelligence.

Secrecy was imposed on the circumstances surrounding the largest loss of life in home waters next to the *Royal Oak*. But as is usually the case with secrecy, where no hard and fast information is to hand, rumours as to the cause of the disaster started to thrive. Many rumours, theories and opinions survive to this day.

Was the loss of *Dasher* the result of an enemy mine? Or the work of a U-boat torpedo? Was it a case of friendly fire where a stray torpedo from a British ship in the busy Clyde waters caught the unfortunate *Dasher*? Whispers were heard of an act of sabotage—perhaps a bomb had been planted when the ship had been in Belfast? Perhaps the cause was a mundane one—the ship's engine blown up or an electrical fault in the lighting system. After all, the operational and mechanical record of the *Dasher*, a recently converted cargo ship, had not been good. Several shortcomings had been all too evident in her short life in commission as an aircraft carrier. Alternatively it was suggested a crew member had been smoking during refuelling of aircraft. Some witnesses also encouraged the view that the explosion occurred when a plane crash landed onto the ship.

Whatever the true reason for the catastrophe, the effect on the lives of three hundred and seventy nine of the crew of HMS *Dasher*

*(Opposite) First photographs of the sea disaster, taken from the bridge of the radar training ship, HMS* Isle of Sark

was terminal. Countless relatives were bereaved for reasons some are still not clear of to this day. Those who witnessed such horrific waste of human life from the island of Arran and from the communities, most notably the town of Ardrossan, on the Ayrshire coast were irredeemably affected by their closeness to disaster.

For the first time since that fateful afternoon in wartime, this book seeks to put together the story. Many survivors and others whose lives were touched by the *Dasher* disaster at the distance of fifty years have been only too glad to take part and bear witness.

Isle of Sark's *lifeboats rescuing survivors from the sea*

# Chapter 2

# Survivors' First Hand Accounts

## Able Seaman Harold Martin

I was in the quarter messdeck when the terrific explosion occurred. Suddenly all the lights went out and sparks flew across the messdeck. I went up an iron ladder and reached the hangar which was like an inferno. Others were turning back but I went through a bulkhead door which was awash.

The ship was going down very fast and there was no time to free any life boats or floats. So it was just a matter of going into the water. I went over the side with a very good friend of mine. His name was Bush. I don't know what happened to him as I never saw him again.

I was in the water for quite some time before being picked up by our 'crash boat'. From then on, our biggest concern was that the loss of ship would be broadcast over the radio, before we could let our parents and wives know that we were all right. However we need not have worried because the whole catastrophe was covered in secrecy and nothing was ever divulged about what had happened.

## Petty Officer John Mann

When I heard the loud bang I opened the watertight door and went forward onto the catwalk along with three lads from 816 Squadron. I could feel the ship was sinking and then I heard the order, Abandon Ship! Abandon Ship!

Flight Sergeant Grieves said, Right lads, let's go. He then leapt over the side and I followed him into the water. I managed to keep afloat until a Carley float went past.

It was absolutely packed. However one of the lads moved to one side and pulled me on board. I looked for the three lads who were with me on the ship, the three lads from 816 Squadron. But they had perished.

In the distance we could see a coaster heading for us and many of those aboard the Carley float jumped into the water and swam towards it. More and more left the Carley float until there were only two of us left on it. I stayed on it because I could not swim.

I saw the coaster picking up some of those in the water and soon she came alongside the Carley float and took the two of us on board. I was very surprised and deeply disappointed to find out that only half of those who had jumped off the Carley float were on board the coaster. The rest had perished.

## J Raynam

All but one of our aircraft had been stowed in the hangar when we went for a short teabreak. We then returned to the flight deck and started to walk to the remaining plane when there was a loud booming noise followed by flames and smoke. The flight deck started to crinkle like corrugated cardboard. Three of us started to couple up the firehoses when the order Abandon Ship! came over the tannoy.

I made my way to my cabin but all the lights were out so I retraced my steps back to the flight deck. A friend of mine who had survived the sinking of HMS *Courageous* started telling me that on that occasion some were lost because they had drifted too far away. I moved forward to where we usually went down the gangway and stepped into the water.

I swam away from the ship in case it sucked me under and joined a bunch of young officers and lads who were pushing planks and other floating objects to anyone in need.

We were all taking things in our stride and there was much banter between us. We watched as the ship pointed to the sky and slipped slowly under. Suddenly up came a pall of smoke and flames. The flames raced across the water in our direction and I swam as fast as possible. I knew that I was swimming for my life. The flames came nearer and nearer—they were so close that I was scared.

After some time in the water, I was picked up by a life boat from the *Isle of Sark*. As they were hauling me aboard the rope slipped from my hands as they were covered in oil and I landed back in the water. I heard a voice say, It's all right, I've got you. At that point I blacked out.

I was taken to Kilmacolm Hydro Hotel which was being used as a naval hospital. Whilst recuperating, the night nurse had to waken me as I was having nightmares about the flames reaching me.

# Lieutenant Commander E W E Lane

I was on the bridge and checking the charts. A course had been shaped for Greenock and a signal was made to lower the boom-net at the Tail o' the Bank, with our ETA (estimated time of arrival) being eighteen hundred hours.

I was about to write down what I was doing when the ship shuddered aft, accompanied by a loud bang.

The officer of the watch pointed to the aircraft lift shaft perfectly horizontal, sailing away fifty feet above the flight deck. To try and find out what was happening I went down onto the first deck and made my way to the second deck along the port alleyway. The ship was in darkness with smoke and debris everywhere. I heard water pouring in and I looked down a hatch to see three feet of water on the third deck.

As the ship was going down by the stern I quickly made my way to the upper deck but by then water was coming over the upper deck level. I crawled forward and went over the side as the ship rapidly settled by the stern until she finally disappeared beneath the flat calm sea.

As I swam in the water I went from Carley float to Carley float shouting, Don't worry, lads. It will be all right. I wanted to boost the morale of those in the water and on the floats. On being rescued from the cold water by a coaster I was transferred to our own motor launch and taken to Ardrossan harbour, then to the Eglinton Hotel.

*(Opposite) Lieutenant Commander E Lane*

## Able Seaman Tom Hunter

I was reading a book and glancing up now and then to watch the progress of a game of 'Uckers' which some of the lads were playing. Suddenly there was a big explosion and all the lights went out. We had an emergency lamp hanging by the watertight door and someone turned it on.

There were two ways out of our mess deck—one was a ladder leading up to the torpedo flat; the other way out was blocked by fire. We all formed an orderly queue to go through the watertight door. From the explosion to going through the door was probably about two minutes. I remember going through just ahead of 'Pincher' Martin. That short period between the explosion and getting the door open seemed like a lifetime.

When we did manage to get the door open, we did not know if the passageway would be on fire or under water. However it was clear of both, but the T124X mess deck was a complete disaster. On going up a ladder, there were bullets exploding from the belts of the machine guns, bullets which were used by our aircraft. A torpedo had broken loose from its moorings and was sliding about.

On reaching the cafeteria it was found to be in a complete mess and there was a huge hole in the deck plates and flames were shooting out. There was a door which had been blown off. I crawled through and made my way to the deck amidst debris, smoke and flames.

Standing on the deck I started to loosen my money belt which contained £3 as we had been paid that very day. I threw the money belt into the water and started to remove my trousers. However my mate, Pincher told me to keep my trousers on, as they would keep me warm whilst I was in the water.

As I stood on the flight deck I saw another of my mates

and I shouted, Are you going over, Gunner? He replied, I cannot swim. That was the last I saw of him. There was absolutely nothing we could throw over the side to help the non-swimmers. By this time the water was almost around our chests and we floated off. Not one of us had lifebelts.

The ship was still going down and as the tide was in my favour, I made hastily away as far as possible before she went under. After a few moments I began to tread water to allow me to look at *Dasher*. She was poised to go down by the stern and was almost vertical. Men were still jumping over and I saw one man dive from an incredible height. Then the ship slipped beneath the waves. It was a sight that I will never forget.

A few minutes later the sea caught fire and I swam very very quickly from the blaze. I swam so fast that I started to get tired. The water was choppy and cold and for some reason or other I thought of the time in Hoboken New York. I was below deck watching a thousand tons of ballast being lowered and when the job was complete I stood and watched a welder with his torch. He welded a steel plate over the hole where the pig iron had gone. He then welded the letters, RIP. If he could only know what was happening at that moment. My thoughts also went to the time I was standing on the flight deck and a huge sheet of flame came out the funnel. Things were so bad with *Dasher*'s boilers that the American shipyard workers refused to work in the engine room.

I was completely on my own in the water. I heard many cries for help but could not see anyone. A small coaster was steaming about half a mile away and the sight of it renewed my energy. However as it approached me its speed did not falter and it went straight past me and headed for the area of sea which had been on fire. I realised that they had made the right decision as those men were in a very poor state.

I heard a voice calling my name and as I went up on a

small wave, I saw Pincher Martin and another rating. They were clinging to a piece of timber which was about twelve feet long and I swam over to them and held on. Pincher dipped his finger into the sea and said he could taste fuel and it was time to make a move. We swam together, away from the fuel and we came across another rating who was not doing very well. We draped him over the timber and kept swimming. After a while we saw a motor launch come alongside and we scrambled up the nets. On being hauled aboard someone started to pump water out of me and I passed out. The next thing I knew, I was in a bunk with just a blanket over me. As I looked round I saw Pincher and Slinger opposite me in bunks. There were smiles and greetings all round and then we were given a large tot of rum which was greatly appreciated.

Although *Dasher* had an inglorious end, she did some good work whilst she was in commission. I will always remember her as a happy ship, even although she was virtually a floating time bomb.

*(Opposite)  Able Seaman Tom Hunter*

## Daniel Gaffney

We were in the Clyde estuary. The aircraft were practising take-off and landing, probably in training for a big operation. I had joined the ship three weeks before in Dundee.

Those of the crew who were on leave that Saturday night were getting themselves ready to go ashore. I had no leave due so I was sitting about playing cards in the mess deck.

Suddenly we heard an explosion, the lights went out and the ship took a violent list. There were about seven of us in the mess deck and the only way out was through a steel door. The steel door was jammed by the sudden movement of the ship.

Four of us took it in turn to try and wrench it open, but failed. I thought to myself, We're done for. Everyone was afraid but there was no panic.

The ship seemed to straighten up and the door suddenly swung open. We could hear everything being loosened from their bearings by the action of the ship. We were two decks down. This meant we had to find our way along an alleyway to a ladder. On our way we met others all making for a way out.

One man who must have lost control was running the opposite way, back into the ship. We collided and I got his head in my face. I was stunned for a minute but managed to hold on to a handrail and keep going. As the ship was rising at the bow, we were virtually walking uphill.

Anything that was moveable was flying around and half of the ship was under water. I reached the deck with a boy who had been playing cards with me. He was on his first trip and he was about my age, 23.

When we reached the side of the ship, we were about sixty feet in the air. My friend said he could not jump that height and I told him he would have to. He was holding onto a chain that ran right round the ship, but by persuasion and some force I got him to jump with me.

I went down very deep in the water and did not seem to be getting up as fast as I should. Probably the ship was pulling me down, for by this time she was sinking. I got my back against the side of the ship and pushed myself up.

I was gasping for breath by the time I reached the surface. I pushed my feet against the hull and swam as strongly as I could to get away from her. When I turned round, the ship was almost under. I hit against a piece of wood and hung on to it for a few minutes whilst I looked around me.

I saw a lot of heads in the water. By this time the ship was gone. There was a raft about one hundred yards away and I swam towards it. When I was halfway to the raft I saw a man floating in the water. He was wearing a life jacket and his face was submerged in the water. I pulled his face out of the water and swam towards a raft whilst holding on to him. On reaching it I told one of the men on the raft to hold onto him, as he was going unconscious. An airman and I then swam out to another man who was in trouble and managed to bring him alongside the raft.

Then with a almighty Whoosh, the sea went on fire. The raft was just outside the fire which was spread over a large area. Those of us who were in the water had to kick our feet to push the raft away, otherwise we would probably have drifted into the flames.

Those survivors who were in the water nearer the ship were burned.

We were in the water for about an hour. During this time an aeroplane flew over us. There was a French sloop and an old coal boat in the vicinity but they could not come near because of the fire. We had to go to them.

There were a lot of men on the raft and not so many hanging on and propelling the raft with our feet towards the rescue ships. Just before we reached the French sloop, I was almost dragged under with its propellers. However I managed to swim clear. They threw a net for us and we managed to struggle aboard.

After an hour and a half, we berthed at Ardrossan. There were a great number of ambulances waiting and we were asked if we wanted to go to hospital. I said no and I was taken to a barracks in Ardrossan where we were given plenty to drink, probably to counteract the shock.

## Petty Officer Reginald Dickens

I was in the hangar with starboard watch and port watch. We had just secured three Swordfish in the after end of the hangar. I detailed starboard watch to go below and port watch to refuel the Hurricanes and Swordfish in the hangar.

As I was walking forward a violent explosion hit me in the back and threw me forward. I saw the after end of the hangar was an inferno and I could see daylight through the deckhead where the aircraft lift should have been.

I realised that the explosion had ripped through the Fleet Air Arm mess deck where my starboard watch were with many of their shipmates. As I made my way through the forward door to the flight deck the flames were red and there was dense smoke.

The ship seemed quite steady and I went down to the quarter deck. By this time the stern was going down. I gave a hand in trying to turn the boats out but this was hopeless. I heard the order, Cast Loose the Carley Floats, then the order Abandon Ship! Abandon Ship!

I could hear the grinding of metal and the crashes within the ship. I jumped over the port side, as soon as the Carley floats hit the water. After floundering about I held onto a Carley float until I was rescued by a coaster and put ashore at Ardrossan where I was well looked after by the locals.

# Sub Lt John Ferrier

I was a member of HMS *Peregrine,* a lease-lend ship from the Americans. We sailed her from Cape Town to Baltimore as the Americans wanted the vessel returned. With some of the Peregrine crew I travelled by train to New York to join HMS *Dasher* which was berthed in the US Navy yard, Brooklyn. There was a great rush to finish the ship. We took her over in an unfinished condition and without a stabilising test having been carried out.

I was a member of *Dasher's* crew throughout her seven months career. Towards the end of March 1943 we were anchored at the Tail o' the Bank, Greenock. Whilst at anchor we were loaded with thousands of tons of pig iron—this ballast was to help the ship's stability. After loading we sailed to Lamlash Bay.

We were involved on the 27th March in deck landing practice. I was on duty on the flight deck with Sub Lt Buxton and Acting Sub Lt Frank Tetlow. Deck landing practice had finished and the three of us were admiring the view of the hills of Arran with the sun behind them. They were so impressed with the scenic beauty that Frank said, When all this is over we are going to visit this part of the country. It is so scenic.

Just then the captain announced over the tannoy that shore leave was being granted when we reached Greenock in one hour's time. I went below deck to my cabin to have a wash and to change into my dress uniform. I then went into the cabin next door to tell Bob Wanless my latest jokes. Sub Lt Tetlow was in the cabin with us.

Suddenly there was a loud explosion. The lights went out and we ran down the corridor which was in darkness. There was another explosion, much louder than the first.

On reaching the deck, which was now at a very steep

*Sub Lieutenant John Ferrier (third from left)*

angle, I met with fellow Greenock man John McFarlane. There were now four of us grouped together—Tetlow, Buxton, John and myself. The angle of the ship was very steep. It was going down fast by the stern.

John McFarlane shouted, What will we do? Having been aboard a ship that had been torpedoed six months before, I had no hesitation in shouting, I'll show you. With that, I took off my jacket and jumped overboard. John did likewise. I am not a very good swimmer and on reaching the surface I saw a biscuit tin which contained 'hard tack'. The tin must have come off one of our lifeboats. I swam towards the biscuit tin and clung to it.

*Dasher* was by now slipping beneath the surface. The bow was very high in the air. I could hear those still on board below deck, screaming as the ship went down. It was terrible.

There were crewmen all around me in the water. Suddenly without any warning there was a loud Whoosh! and the sea was on fire. It must have been the aviation fuel.

The sea of fire trapped many of the men. One minute they had been swimming and the next minute they were encircled in searing flames. They were shouting and screaming. I could feel the heat from the flames as I clung onto my biscuit tin. It was awful hearing those screams and watching the men being burned, being burned to death.

The screaming stopped. Thick oil was everywhere. We were all covered in black fuel oil from *Dasher*'s fuel storage tanks—seventy five thousand gallons of thick black oil.

I was rescued by a coaster which had picked up some other survivors and we were transferred to HMS *Sir Galahad*. Aboard this minesweeper there were many survivors and some bodies.

My friend from Greenock did not survive even although he was a good swimmer. It is possible that the had struck his head on *Dasher* when he surfaced after jumping off the ship.

## E W Cane

I joined *Dasher* in Brooklyn Navy yard and I was aboard when we gave cover to several Atlantic convoys, and also when we joined other ships of the fleet for Operation Overlord to assist in the invasion of North Africa.

We were assigned as escort carrier to a Russian convoy in one of the fjords of Iceland, but during the early part of the voyage suffered damage to the hull during a storm in mountainous seas, forcing us to leave the convoy and return to Dundee for repairs.

After completing a refit at Dundee we proceeded to the Clyde for working up trials, including the flying on of a new squadron.

On the afternoon of 27th March 1943 we had been at flying stations giving pilots landing practice and receiving on board the new squadron. Flying operations were completed during late afternoon and we stood down. Being non-duty watch that evening, I proceeded to the mess to wash and change ready for a run ashore that evening.

This however was not to be, for whilst proceeding up the Clyde there was a terrific explosion at the after end of the ship, which was immediately followed by the whole vessel being plunged into total darkness. Fortunately, having been on board since commissioning, the layout of the stairways and ladders were familiar to me and I made my way to the upper deck. Self-preservation must have been uppermost in my mind, for I do not recall meeting or having any other persons with me on the journey to the upper deck.

On reaching the fo'c'sle I joined a PO (whom I now know was Jeff Gray) and three or four other ratings in releasing and throwing overboard a number of Carley floats. During the three or four minutes we were carrying out this procedure, three bulkheads collapsed under the pressure of the water and *Dasher* went down further by the stern at each collapse.

It became impossible to control and release any more floats and PO Gray gave us all the go-ahead to jump and save ourselves. On reaching the rails I found that the water was anything up to eighty feet below but this was no time to be scared and as I jumped I saw several others jumping around me.

It seemed ages before I resurfaced but when I did there was not a soul anywhere near me, nor could I see any of the Carley floats we had thrown overboard. Looking around I found the tide had taken me some thirty or more yards away from the ship which was now at an even more vertical angle. Remembering stories of the suction created by ships when sinking, I struck out to swim as far away from the hull as possible. I watched *Dasher* go under from some distance but felt no 'pull' from her.

Shortly after I was hauled on board a Carley float by a coder, a fellow member of the communications mess whose name I am unable to recall. How long I was in the water is impossible to tell but I know that it felt like an age.

The float by this time could hold no more survivors as we had an injured rating on board, but at least two others swam towards us and held on to the side ropes, one being the yeoman of signals, Nick Carter.

As the coastal vessel approached, that picked us up, it appeared to be bearing down on us at some speed. This was mostly an optical illusion for it was really the tide carrying us towards it. Although both PO Gray and myself shouted to Nick to hang on, he let go of the rope and swam down the port side of the rescue vessel and was lost. As we were being helped aboard and up the scrambling nets, the fire, which was blazing due to diesel oil and aviation spirit which had come to the surface and ignited, hit the port side of the vessel. It was into this inferno that Yeoman Carter swam.

After being given blankets we were taken to the engine room and were able to get out of our wet clothes. It was here that I was fortunate enough to find my best friend Eric Hayward (Sig TO) with whom I had spent many happy times ashore during the period we were in New York.

We were allowed to make one telephone call to inform our next of kin of our safe survival. One of the last acts in this most tragic event which left a lasting impression on me was the slow march to the cemetery at Ardrossan alongside the vehicles carrying the coffins.

*Ordinary Signalman Eddie Cane (1942)*

## Tom Dawson

I was on duty as wheel man in the wheel house with the Bosun's mate, Danny McCartney. Suddenly there was a dull thud and all the lights flashed for about thirty seconds. Then all went off and there was complete silence.

I shouted up the voice-pipe to the bridge, reporting what had happened. Then sent Danny out on deck to investigate and stayed at my post with my hands firmly on the wheel.

As I looked ahead, I glanced at the paper cut-out which Russel Brockbank had given me. I had pinned it onto the bulkhead from a piece of string. Danny returned and said, I think the ship is going down by the stern. At that point I noticed the paper cut-out was coming away from the bulkhead. I then said, I think we ought to go!

Danny and I jumped into the water but when we surfaced, I became tangled in a rope and it took me some time to free myself. Meantime Danny was swimming away completely unaware of my predicament. I then swam to a flotanet. Holding onto it was my friend, Danny (with twelve others). The ship's navigator was shouting for help with someone in trouble. I swam over but the shipmate was already dead.

Just then the sea caught fire and I swam away from the flames as fast as I could. I realised that I was very cold, my senses were gradually dulling, my arms and legs were moving very slowly and I became disinterested in what was happening. As I was hauled aboard a Carley float, I lost consciousness and came to three hours later aboard the *Isle of Sark*. One of its crew was rubbing me vigorously with a towel. The last I saw of my friend Danny McCartney was when Danny was holding onto a Carley float as the sea caught fire. Danny perished with many of his shipmates.

What I was suffering from in the water is now known as hypothermia.

## Robert McGarvie Dotchin

There was a terrific explosion. I made my way to the flight deck just forward of the bridge on the starboard side. The after end of the flight deck was already in the water, the aircraft lift had been blown up in the air by the force of the explosion. As I arrived on the flight deck a Swordfish aircraft that had been parked at the forward end slid the full length of the deck and into the water.

All the men on the flight deck and the deck below jumped into the water. Jumping from a height of sixty feet knocked the wind out of me and on hitting the water I felt myself being pulled under by the sinking ship.

After what seemed like an eternity I surfaced and found myself close to the bow which was the only part of the ship that remained above water. I saw a 'flotanet' with its lashings still on and rotating in the water. Men were trying to catch hold of a rope. I swam towards the 'flotanet' with about a dozen of my shipmates and we all managed to hold on.

The sea was quite calm but cold. Shortly after we had caught hold of the float a large bubble erupted about twenty yards away and immediately the sea was on fire. It burned so fiercely that we could feel the heat. We held on to our float and managed to propel it away from the fire. We could hear the men who were trapped in the fire shouting and screaming. After a while the shouting and screaming stopped.

After floating for some time a large open boat arrived and started to pull us on board. Shortly before it got there a few of the lads slipped under, no doubt from exhaustion and the cold.

We remained at Ardrossan until after the funeral of my shipmates who were laid to rest at the local cemetery. On returning from survivor's leave I was sent to HMS *Osprey* at Dunoon as part of the anti submarine branch.

The most traumatic part of the whole experience was after receiving letters from the families of some of the men who had perished, I had to visit them. They had been told by the Admiralty that their sons were Missing Presumed Lost. I think that was the cruelest thing of all. I knew that if the men had not been picked up by the next day, they never would be. Their relatives could not understand the situation.

*Robert McGarvie Dotchin (July 1942)*

## Sub Lt Lionel Godfrey RNVR

891 Squadron

Four of our Hurricanes, their pilots and almost all of the squadron's maintenance personnel had been taken aboard by lighter. The following day, Max Newman, myself and two other pilots were circling the carrier as she worked up speed into wind, preparatory to us landing when *Dasher* exploded before our eyes and sank from view within four minutes. In my mind's eye I can still see the lift being hurled some two to three hundred feet into the air and bodies falling from its surface into the sea.

There was nothing we could do except keep radio silence and return to Machrihanish. Two days later I ended up taking compulsory leave in London. At no time since the tragic end of HMS *Dasher* have I heard of or seen an official acknowledgement of her loss.

After four week's leave without pay and without notice of an appointment back on duty I visited a branch of the Admiralty in Queen Anne's Mansions, London in an endeavour to learn what I should do with myself. From a Commander seated behind a desk I received a flat denial that anything untoward had happened to *Dasher* or to 891 Squadron. When I, a mere Sub Lieutenant protested that with my own eyes I'd seen *Dasher* go down and disappear beneath the calm waters of the Firth of Clyde, the only response I got from the severe looking Commander was , Nonsense! You'd better go and get yourself a casual payment and remain on indefinite leave.

CHAPTER 3

# BEARING WITNESS

The escort aircraft carrier HMS *Dasher* was officially noted as having sunk at 16.48 on the afternoon of 27th March 1943. This was a mere six minutes after the recorded time of the explosion on board. This ship with her crew of over five hundred, her defence compliment of some fifteen aircraft, her store of fuel, weapons and equipment—all vanished from view. Wartime conditions of secrecy required that not a word of the event should be communicated to the enemy for fear of ceding some advantage, however slight, in the tactical battle of the North Atlantic supply routes.

How could the *Dasher*'s sad demise be noticed? Who could have seen it? Who could have heard of it? How could it be remembered?

It is perhaps difficult for the modern reader to conceive of wartime conditions of the River Clyde estuary. Trade at that time was brisk and Clyde ports turned over a massive tonnage of cargo to and from all parts of the globe. The years of the Second World War intensified maritime activity on the river. Military cargoes alone handled by Clyde docks at this time totalled 3.17 million tons. During the years of hostilities between 1939 and 1945 shipyards from Glasgow to Greenock were recorded as having built 1903 naval and merchant

51

vessels. A massive 23191 vessels were counted as having been repaired or refitted in Clyde yards and a further 637 were subject to conversion work. In 1943 alone, over one million Americans came to the Clyde. A total of some 4.95 million troops were counted as having passed through the ports of Greenock and Gourock during the war years.

River traffic, it is safe to say, was heavy.

Had *Dasher* suffered its grim fate in the remote and inhospitable waters of the North Atlantic, who can say whether any survivors would have lived to tell the tale. Such an event in the waters of the Clyde were never likely to pass without notice.

"Whatever was causing the thick black smoke," junior engineer James Greenhill told me, "must have been visible to even casual observers. My shipmates and I saw a cloud of dense black smoke rising hundreds of feet in the air." James Greenhill's view was from the deck of the SS *City of Venice* anchored at the entrance to Loch Long some fifteen miles to the north. "Any service observers with binoculars," he added, "must have seen the cause in great detail."

The vessels closest to *Dasher* appear to have been *Dasher*'s own *Motor Launch 528*, the destroyer *La Capricieuse*, the radar training ship, HMS *Isle of Sark* and her sister ship, HMS *Attacker*.

The cargo vessel SS *Lithium* owned by Imperial Chemical Industries was also nearby and was able to assist in the rescue to great effect. A report was made to the Naval Control Service Officer, Fleetwood by the master of the *Lithium* on March 30th 1943. This document was of course designated top secret. In it the master reports,

"At 16.42 on Saturday 27th March 1943, whilst on passage from Glasgow to Llanddulas, when in a position S by W1/2W (about 6 miles by log from the Cumbrae Light), we passed Aircraft Carrier *Dasher* 1/4 mile to starboard.

"At this time we observed the Aircraft Carrier blow up—a bright flash appeared from after side amidships, and dense smoke issued from under the Flight Deck.

"We saw the ship was sinking rapidly by the stern—we turned about to render what assistance we could, picking up approximately 60 survivors. These were placed on board HMS *Sir Galahad*. (a Knight class auxiliary minesweeper)

"At 18.30 the ship proceeded on her voyage, after disembarking survivors."

Perhaps the most dramatic human story of the *Dasher* disaster—though only narrowly—concerns the fate of the unfortunate William Macdonald, the seaman who was blown through the hole in the side of ship and landed in the water some four hundred yards away still holding his kitbag.

Leading Sick Berth Attendant Lionel E Banberger relates the story.

"I was aboard *Dasher*'s duty *Motor Launch 528*. We had been circulating our ship in the event of an aircraft over-shooting and landing in the water.

"I was in the wheelhouse at the time of the explosion and I saw the aircraft lift rising high into the sky. I then saw my shipmates jumping overboard.

"As we moved in to carry out a rescue we picked up a seaman who was clutching a kitbag. He was about four hundred yards from *Dasher* and he was practically unconscious. I asked him how he had managed to get in the water so far away from the ship. He replied that he was blown out.

"I put the seaman in the sick bay and asked him his name and he replied, William Macdonald. I made my way forward back on deck and saw *Dasher* going under.

"We picked up another seventeen shipmates out of the water and twenty two out of Carley floats.

"William Macdonald's face, hands and chest were burned and the skin of his hands had been blown off. He spoke coherently and there was no misunderstanding about what he was saying as he had a good hold on himself."

Sadly, after his miraculous exit from the doomed *Dasher*, airman Macdonald survived for a further two weeks before he died of his injuries. He was aged twenty and is buried in Ardrossan cemetery.

Lt Commander G W Dobson RD, RNR was in command of the destroyer *La Capricieuse*.

"We were five miles north-west of *Dasher* when the explosion occurred. As we approached the ship she settled by the stern. I increased speed and had our lifeboats slung out.

"She went down very quickly and finally almost in a vertical position. There was a small ship, the *Cragsman* which became obscured with smoke and I thought that she had been enveloped by the flames in the sea. She was actually there picking up survivors.

"Our lifeboats brought back twenty six survivors. We took them on board and made for Ardrossan. However by the time we had berthed seven of them had died."

Photographs taken from on board the radar training ship *Isle of Sark* provide perhaps the most graphic evidence of the scale and horror of the tragedy. In a completely spontaneous response and against regulations, as he watched the drama unfold, Alex Buchanan, a training instructor photographed the action with his own little box camera.

He explained that at the time of the explosion he was on the bridge of *Isle of Sark*.

"We headed for the scene at full speed and as I had a camera in my hand, I took a photograph immediately of the thick black column of smoke. I took another photograph at a distance of one mile. At this point we could see some life rafts from *Dasher* and survivors in the water. On reaching the scene, we quickly lowered our life boats and they cast off to pluck the survivors from the cold sea.

"We watched as our lifeboats hauled the survivors on board. They also took on board many of *Dasher*'s crew who had perished. When our lifeboats returned, having ensured that they could be of no more assistance, we helped the survivors on board *Isle of Sark*.

We covered them in blankets and took them below deck. Three of them were unconscious and although our crew tried to resuscitate them, they did not regain consciousness.

*Dasher*'s captain and the ship's navigator were among those whom we saved. In total we saved thirty two from the cruel sea."

Arguably the witness, operating in an official capacity with the most uninterrupted and continuous view of events was sitting in an observation hut three hundred feet above in the Arran hills. William McAuslin of the Royal Army Observer Corps had been watching the Swordfish practising landings on *Dasher*'s flight deck.

"The ship changed course towards the mainland and was 'stern on' me when I noticed a huge burst of smoke. A friend who was with me said, Do you think she's all right?

"The carrier seemed to be on an even keel, but suddenly I said, Oh Heavens, she's going! One of her planes slid down the steeply listing flight deck and fell into the sea.

"The ship seemed to stand on end. Then it slowly disappeared before me. The whole thing from the explosion to her final disappearance took only about five minutes.

"I still had my glasses trained on the spot and I saw three rafts on the surface."

The sinking of *Dasher* and the consequent loss of life, the physical injuries and mental scarring suffered by the survivors and the great pain of bereaved relatives was probably no different from many another human disaster before and since. In terms of numbers of casualties from naval accidents and combat encounters in home waters, the experience *of* HMS *Dasher* ranks high.

What added to the suffering of those caught up in this tragedy however, were the conditions of wartime secrecy in force. There had been problems with this converted cargo ship and a feeling expressed by more than one source in my investigations that the conversion was not what it should have been. The account of the *Dasher's* short seven month career in commission in a later chapter point certainly to some shortcomings.

It is in the traditions of all of the armed services that the ultimate sacrifice sometimes has to be made in the cause of a greater gain. The armed services are proud of their traditions of organisation, skill, and courage. Those who pay the ultimate price with their lives are honoured. However it is true to say that wartime secrecy did appear to inhibit the understanding of what happened and the way in which those who survive are able to come to terms with tragedy, recover and then go on.

Petty Officer John B Lawson served on *Dasher's* sister ship, HMS *Attacker*. His testimony is worth recording in full. It brings into sharp focus one of the most dramatic elements of the whole event.

"I served aboard HMS *Attacker*. *Dasher* was supposed to join us in her first convoy from the States to the UK. However she developed engine trouble and some problems with the hydraulics on the aircraft lift. There were other teething troubles—so many in fact, she had to miss the convoy to have them rectified in the States.

"*Attacker* and *Dasher* were involved in Operation Torch, the invasion of North Africa. The next time we saw *Dasher* was in the Clyde, 27th March 1943. We had heard many stories of her being a 'jinx ship'. Attacker was working up for convoy duty. I was on the flight deck when we all heard an almighty explosion. I looked towards the Cumbraes and saw a large column of smoke, then flames appeared. They were very big flames.

"We launched our two whalers and they rowed towards the area. Action Stations! was announced on board *Attacker* and everybody went to their respective posts. I was on duty in Damage Control in the hangar and as I made my way there I looked towards the black smoke and flames. The flames covered an area about half a mile square. Many rescue vessels were heading for the area.

"We were all very wary, thinking it a torpedo or a mine. Also if it could happen to *Dasher*, it could happen to us. While I was in the hangar, I kept a wary eye on the exit doors, in case I had to make a quick exit.

"On the whalers' return, the officer of the day took the oarsmen straight to the captain's office. Later signals were passed to all ships in the vicinity that 'The incident is not, repeat not, to be spoken about.'

"We heard through the ships' grapevine that our whalers had picked up many survivors and transferred them to a Royal Navy vessel. Having been ordered not to speak about the disaster, we never ever spoke about it."

The incident is not to be spoken about. We never ever spoke about it. In the light of what has been learned about coping with disasters in recent years, for those who survived and those who were bereaved, this order and the obedient response to it we now know was probably the worst advice to give. It certainly would have added to the burden of grief and shock experienced by all.

At Ardrossan Harbour the distress signal was received and action was taken immediately. All home based minesweepers were to proceed to the disaster area with the utmost speed and assist in the rescue operation.

One of the timber built minesweepers berthed at HMS *Fortitude* (the wartime name for Ardrossan harbour), Number 23, put to sea immediately. The fact that only one third of the crew were aboard did not deter the captain from proceeding to the assistance of *Dasher*'s unfortunate crew.

The activity at Ardrossan harbour and the sudden departure of all ships alerted the residents in the near vicinity and some made their way to the top of the high ground above the town, 'Cannon Hill'. Here local people were able to witness the dramatic events. Although by no stretch of the imagination could they visualise the appalling conditions the hundreds of seamen were suffering as they struggled for survival.

When the explosion was heard on the south beach promenade between Ardrossan and Saltcoats, the strollers paused and looked westwards out to sea. As the shipyard buildings hid the disaster from their view, a huge thick pall of smoke was all they could see.

As the locals watched, the words, 'an exercise' were carried along the promenade. An exercise? Ah well, they have to practise, I suppose, a dismal Johnny was heard to say.

Slowly the strollers moved on. After all it seemed reasonable that the present wartime conditions, a naval vessel might be engaged in firing practice and putting up a smoke screen. Our local strollers made their way home as tea-time was approaching and the navy exercise was of little concern to them.

The local cinemas were all running films, including the propaganda reels, to packed audiences who were completely unaware of the drama unfolding just offshore. They were soon to become involved as each of the four cinemas flashed a message onto the screens. The message was: ALL CIVIL DEFENCE AND FIRST AID PERSONNEL REPORT TO POSTS IMMEDIATELY!

The first ambulance to arrive at the harbour was driven by Harry Judd. He watched as the rescue flotilla arrived. The first to berth was *La Capricieuse* followed by *ML 528* and then the first of the home based minesweepers.

When Harry Judd's ambulance was packed with the badly burned sailors, it was despatched to the Royal Navy Sick Bay in South Crescent Ardrossan. On the way there the ambulance passed the ever growing fleet of first aid vehicles with doctors, nurses and stretcher bearers.

In addition to conventional ambulances, there were a number of ambulance trailers. These consisted of a metal chassis mounted on two car wheels and were capable of carrying up to six stretcher cases. Their sides consisted of waterproof canvas which could be rolled up to enable the stretcher cases to be strapped in. The canvas would then be rolled down and tied in position.

A gruesome sight was witnessed by many as one of the ambulance trailers turned a corner. A limp arm appeared from under the canvas and dangled over the side of the trailer with the hand trailing along the road. The driver of the speeding vehicle pulling the ambulance trailer was completely unaware of this most unfortunate circumstance of one of *Dasher*'s casualties in his charge.

The ambulances took the casualties to four separate destinations—

the Royal Navy Sick Bay at 8 South Beach, Ardrossan;
the first aid post in Saltcoats;
Ballochmyle Hospital, thirty miles south of Ardrossan;
and the morgue at Ardrossan's Harbour Street.

Those not requiring medical attention were taken to the Royal Navy base in Glasgow Street. The officers were taken to the Eglinton Hotel in Ardrossan's Princess Street.

The ratings were billeted with the locals of Ardrossan and between seven and ten days later, the officers were moved from the Eglinton Hotel into accommodation with locals. During their stay in Ardrossan, in keeping with orders, not one survivor spoke to any local about any part of the tragedy.

On that fateful day which the residents of Ardrossan will never forget, the bodies of nineteen of *Dasher*'s crew were brought ashore. The first signal to HMS *Fortitude* that day had been PREPARE FOR A LARGE NUMBER OF CASUALTIES. This large number was reflected in the huge fleet of approximately fifty ambulances and ambulance trailers that arrived at the harbour. Many of them returned to their base that night as they were classed as 'not required'. Out of *Dasher*'s crew of 528, the 'large number' that in fact made it alive to the shore totalled 149.

The loss of life was comprised as follows—
  Royal Navy       346
  Merchant Navy    27
  Royal Air Force  3
  NAAFI            3
  The total loss of the ship's company amounted to 379 men.

---

Officers Killed, Brought Ashore
Buxton, Trevor Victor          Ty Act Sub Lt (E) RNVR
Haughie, William Pratt         Ty Act Sub Lt (E) RNVR
Stallard-Penoyre, Ralph Carnac Baker   Lt RN
McFarlane J                    Ty Sub Lt


Ratings Killed, Brought Ashore
Costar, Ernest C          Able Seaman        C/JX.190282
Craig, Archibald B        Leading Seaman
                                        RDF P/JX.212188
Crawford, James           Diesel Greaser          T.124.X
Davis, Cecil J            Ordinary Telegraphist
                                        C/JX.271890
Gillies, William          Leading Writer Temporary
                                        D/SR.16610
Harper, Harry             Able Seaman        C/JX.260671
Kane, James               Able Seaman        C/SSX.18806
Lawrence, Arthur C        Diesel Greaser          T124.X
Liddle, Richard           Ordinary Seaman    C/JX.374403
Martin, Thomas            Able Seaman        C/JX.168035
Melville, John            Ordinary Coder     C/JX.361352
Neath, Ronald             Leading Radio Mechanic
                                        P/MX.100601
Percival, George H M      Ordinary Seaman    C/JX.359516
Woolaghan, Sylvester      Able Seaman        C/JX.212950
Wright, Jack S            Able Seaman         C/J.110766

---

As the sun went down behind the Arran hills bringing this day of disaster to a close, what was there on the sea to show the horror of what had happened? Amazingly life goes on and the traffic of trade and of war resumed as normal. Out there on the Clyde after night fell the vessel *Lady Dorothy* plied southwards over the point of the disaster.

Retired captain Archie Murchie of Ardrossan tells the story in full.

"I was on duty as chief officer aboard this Nobel Explosives Company vessel, the *Lady Dorothy*, which was specially adapted to carry high explosives such as dynamite, cordite and nitro-glycerine. We had loaded up with twenty one thousand cases of high explosives, in total two hundred and fifty tons from the three explosive store ships which were anchored in Loch Riddon.

"We sailed south, keeping strictly to the mineswept channel. Due to our cargo we were never allowed to join a convoy. I was on the bridge with Captain James Gemmell, who like myself was an Ardrossan man. At a point in our voyage almost midway between Ardrossan and Brodick I noticed that the sea was deadly calm, without so much as a ripple and I mentioned this to the captain. We then noticed some wreckage and flotsam. At that point the captain turned to me and said, Take a closer look.

"I noted that the time was 8.00pm. I made my way starboard and descended down a Jacob's ladder. I shone my torch into the water and saw thick oil. I put my hand into the oil and noted that it was several inches thick—in fact about three inches. That would account for the sea being so calm.

"On returning to the bridge I reported to the captain that a ship had either been torpedoed or mined. Due to the strict black-out we could not switch on our searchlights and there were no other ships in the vicinity. It appeared that any life-saving operation had ceased. We therefore continued on our voyage to the north west of England."

When Archie Murchie returned to Ardrossan, he picked up local talk about the sinking. He often thinks of that fateful day and what they would have done with their own deadly cargo if they had been passing just three hours earlier.

When the bodies were received in Ardrossan the next of kin were informed of the loss and they travelled to the town. Waiting to meet them were local residents who were there to offer the bereaved relatives support, sympathy and free accommodation.

When the trains stopped at Ardrossan railway station it was not difficult to identify the relatives as they were dressed in black and they could not hide their grief.

On meeting with Royal Navy personnel, the bereaved relatives were informed that

> "An explosion took place on board, when the ship was in company with other vessels who rendered every assistance that was possible to save lives."

Of the deceased brought ashore, three were buried in their home towns. Twelve were accorded full naval honours at a funeral in Ardrossan. There appeared to have been some contention over the funeral arrangements. The expectation of the navy was clearly that the deceased would be buried in unmarked graves in Ardrossan. It appeared the requirement for secrecy was felt necessary to carry on to the grave.

Acting Sub Lieutenant John McFarlane was dead on arrival at Ardrossan. The Royal Navy wanted to bury him in the joint funeral service in Ardrossan. However his father demanded the body as he wanted his son buried in the family lair in Greenock. After much raising of voices between the father and the officer in charge, it was agreed that the deceased could be buried in accordance with his father's wishes. John McFarlane was buried in Lair 188, a family lair, which is in Section 3P of Greenock Cemetery. His funeral was on 2nd April 1943. Another six crewmen are buried in Greenock.

For the Ardrossan ceremony the coffins, each draped with the Union Jack, rested on an open backed lorry. There were six highly

*The* Lady Dorothy *sailed over the site of the disaster three hours later. She was loaded with high explosives*

**TELEGRAM**

Charges to pay
RECEIVED

POST 164 7DY CHMS

No.
OFFICE STAMP
GALASHIELS

Prefix. Time handed in. Office of Origin and Service Instructions. Words.

12-19 .m   57
From E H Mn:   57 10.10 7DY CHMS 36   To

MRS E MELVILL 164 WOOD ST GALASHIELS SELKIRKSHIRE

= DEEPLY REGRET TO REPORT DEATH OF YOUR HUSBAND LETTER

FOLLOWS FUNERAL ARRANGEMENTS WILL COMMUNICATED DIRECT

TO YOU BY FLAG OFFICER IN CHARGE GREENOCK =

COMMODORE ROYAL NAVAL BKS CHATHAM +

For free repetition of doubtful words telephone " TELEGRAMS ENQUIRY " or call, with this form
at office of delivery. Other enquiries should be accompanied by this form, and, if possible, the envelope

R.N. Barracks,
Chatham.

29th March, 1943.

Dear Madam,

In confirmation of the telegram already sent
to you, I deeply regret to have to inform you that
your husband, John Melville, (Ordinary Coder,
C/JX.361352), has been killed while on war service
on 27th March 1943.

Please allow me, on behalf of the officers and
men of the Royal Navy, the high traditions of which
your husband helped to maintain, to express my
sincere sympathy with you in your sad bereavement.

I am, Madam,

Yours sincerely,

Commodore.

Mrs. E. Melville,
164 Wood Street,
Galashiels,
Selkirkshire.

polished lorries each carrying two coffins.

Immediately behind were the relatives of the deceased, in cars provided by the Royal Navy. The cars were followed by the firing party and then a naval band as well as a large representation of the Royal Navy and the Women's Royal Navy Service.

At the head of the procession was Captain J L Field who gave the order, Slow March!

Slowly the cortege proceeded along Glasgow Street, passing the shops that had closed for the day due to the distressing circumstances. The solemn proceedings were watched in respectful silence by a very large crowd of spectators. One lady in the crowd was so impressed by the highly organised and dignified procession that she was heard to say, It's like a Royal funeral. At Eglinton school the children were allowed out of their classrooms to enable them to pay their last respects.

On reaching the cemetery in Sorbie Road, the twelve bodies were laid to rest. As each coffin was lowered, a volley of shots was fired by the firing party.

For some weeks afterwards debris and oil were washed ashore. In 1943 John Sweenie of Townhead, Stevenston was a seven year old boy. He remembers being taken for a walk along the beach between Saltcoats and Ardrossan by his uncle Billy (William Black).

"The water was covered in oil and the beach was littered with birds. The birds could not fly as they were completely covered in oil. Uncle Billy started to catch them and as he caught them he would break their necks to put them out of their misery. We spent a long time on the beach involved in this unpleasant task. Sadly, there was no help available to assist the suffering birds, unlike today."

To prevent material including torpedoes and explosives coming ashore, as well as the bodies of the many deceased, a wire mesh was placed over the wreck.

*(Opposite) Telegram to Mrs E Melville . . . and letter*

A list of those admitted to Ballochmyle Hospital in the
twenty four hours to 28.3.43 revealed that twenty members
of *Dasher*'s crew were receiving medical attention.

William Balfour Addison (43)
    Petty Officer FAA
    RYRB/14494
Barry James Barnett (21)
    1st Class Air Mechanic FAA 816 Sqdn.
    FX/80707
Frederick Thomas Cole (38)
    Asst Steward
    NAP/107711
Ronald Hague (21)
    AB Seaman RDF
    P/JX271957
Arthur Hughes (25)
    AB Seaman LFD
    CJX/155789
Robert Jenkins (31)
    O/TELS
    CJX/250524
Neil Cameron Murray (23)
    Steward
    NAP/R 158176
John Lenard Philips (25)
    Storekeeper
    NAP/R 203519
Edward Rhodes (22)
    AB Seaman
    CJX/258532
Thomas William Townsend (24)
    AB Seaman
    C/OSX 19786

Robert Watts (21)
  AB Seaman
  CJX/158015
William George Caley (27)
  Leading Seaman
  CSSX 26817
Raymond Coles (20)
  AB Seaman
  JX/301801
Eric Richard Hall (20)
  Leading Airman FAA 816 Sqdn.
  FX/89076
Gerard Heeney (32)
  Steward
  APR/35483
William McPherson (32)
  Leading Stoker
  NAP/R 230432
Alfred Norman Penman (22)
  AB Seaman (HMS *Pembroke*)
  CJX/178003
Cledwyn Robinson (23)
  AB Seaman
  CJX/168614
Edward Cyril Trail (31)
  Petty Officer (HMS *Mersey*)
  T/124X
William Albert Wall (32)
  L Writer 891 Sqdn. DN FAA
  P/DX18

## Leading Wren Barbara Kay

"I was attached to the Royal Naval Hospital, Sick Quarters, South Crescent, Ardrossan. This hospital was known as 'Sick Bay' and comprised of a reception area, a medical ward, a surgical ward, an operating theatre and doctors' quarters.

"On Saturday 27th March 1943, Lieutenant Surgeon Kinnett, Lieutenant Surgeon Bulstrade, ambulance driver Harry Judd, two other nurses and I were on duty. We received a telephone call which alerted us to expect a large number of wounded personnel *from a burning ship*. The duty Ambulance driver, Harry Judd left immediately

"We quickly moved the patients who were recuperating into a side room. This would enable us to accommodate up to twenty casualties. As the other staff and I waited for the first ambulance to arrive we spoke of the medical cases which up to now had consisted of appendicitis, piles, scabies and other more or less minor ailments. Anything more seriously wrong and the patient would have been transferred to Ballochmyle Hospital in Mauchline.

"As we were speaking, the first ambulance arrived and we all went quickly out to meet it. I assisted in carrying the stretcher cases into the surgical ward where we found one of them to be dead on arrival. We had no sooner stripped the clothes off the very badly burned sailors when another ambulance arrived. The other Wrens and I once more helped in carrying the severely injured into Sick Bay. We put these patients into the medical ward.

After each operation I had to sterilise the scalpels and other medical equipment.

"Lieutenant Commander E W E Lane RN was brought in. However he was only a little shocked so I gave him a cup of tea. Shortly after he was admitted, when it was made known that he was 'in good health', he was made Officer in Charge,

Identification of Bodies.

"Of the twenty patients admitted, three were found to be dead on arrival. We were kept very busy tending to our seventeen patients who called us by our Christian names when they required anything.

I was selected to represent Sick Bay at the funeral service. It was a very sad occasion."

*(Below) Members of Sick Bay staff, Ardrossan 1943*
*(l to r) Barbara Kay, John Mathison, Joan Chapman & Harry Judd*

*Leading Wren, Barbara Kay, Sick Bay Ardrossan*
*(Inset) Barbara Kay, grandmother*

## Alister McKelvie

Seaview Farm, Corriegills, Brodick, Isle of Arran

"Saturday 27th March 1943 was my eleventh birthday. I was walking through a field to help my parents plant potatoes. My father shouted at me, Something dreadful has happened to that aircraft carrier.

"We did not have a very good view of what was happening but we could see a tremendous amount of black smoke and there was a plane flying over the area.

"I ran over to our neighbours as I knew that from there, I would have a better view. On reaching the house, the two brothers, Dougie and Archie Cook were standing outside. Dougie said to me, It's a terrible tragedy. The water's on fire!

"Dougie had been looking through the binoculars and he handed them to me. I could then see a wall of flame about twenty feet high and colossal black smoke. I could also see some activity at Brodick pier and I made my way down to it.

"On reaching the pier *The Two Boys*, a naval vessel not unlike a fishing boat, was on its way out to the disaster area. I waited about the pier until *The Two Boys* returned. There were no survivors or fatalities aboard and the navy grey paint on the vessel was all blistered with the heat from the burning sea.

"Over the next day or two I made enquiries at Lamlash pier and I was told that like Brodick, no survivors or bodies were recovered by the boats that had departed from Lamlash.

"As there were no reports in the newspapers about the sea tragedy, due to censorship, I always thought that everyone aboard the aircraft carrier had perished. Due to the very sad circumstances I will never forget my eleventh birthday."

## Reg Summerscales

Old Blairbeg, Lamlash, Isle of Arran

"During 1942/43 I was stationed at the Signal Squadron, Kings Cross Point on the Isle of Arran as a signalman, Royal Navy. There was during my period there a lot of 'working up' of new ships. Among them were aircraft carriers which were always heavily involved in deck landing training with their aircraft.

"I was on duty on Saturday 27th March 1943. At 09.00 I watched *Dasher* as she sailed from Lamlash Bay, Isle of Arran to carry out deck landing training. I observed her in the Clyde estuary during the day. At 16.30 *Dasher* called us by the lamp. The signal which I received read—

TO FLAG OFFICER IN COMMAND, GREENOCK
FROM HMS *DASHER*
ESTIMATED TIME OF ARRIVAL, TAIL OF BANK, GREENOCK 18.00 HOURS

"The signal was telephoned to Naval Officer in Command (NOIC), Lamlash for onward teleprinter transmission to Gourock.

"On leaving the telephone I looked out and noticed some smoke coming from *Dasher* astern below the flight deck and I informed Naval Officer in Command, Lamlash. At first I thought that an aircraft had crashed but she had recovered all her aircraft.

I tried to contact *Dasher* by lamp but I received no reply. Soon after she disappeared stern first, amid smoke.

"I was ordered to Keep the *Dasher* Incident Quiet and Never Repeat Anything Which I Had Witnessed.

"Little did I know in 1943 that the loss of life would be so great and it was not until 1991 that I ascertained the very high number who had perished."

*Signalman Reg Summerscales received the last signal from* Dasher
*requesting the boom net be lowered at the Tail o' the Bank. As he received
the message he noticed smoke from the stern of the ship.*
*(Inset) Reg Summerscales (1994)*

## Malcolm L MacKenzie

"I was a boy of ten years living with my family at Farmfield Farm Cottage, West Kilbride. My father was a Lieutenant, RNVR attached to HMS *Fortitude* at Ardrossan harbour.

"The afternoon of 27th March 1943 was fair and calm. At the time of the incident I was on Law Hill. Although shipping movements in the Clyde at that time were plentiful, the sight of an aircraft carrier was rare and I was watching the progress of the vessel. In fact I had a perfect panorama of the whole scene.

"The explosion came as a low thudding sound with thick smoke quickly rising from the ship. She settled and sank in very quick time and I recall the deep feeling of sadness knowing that men must have died. Many small vessels put out from Ardrossan, Fairlie and Arran ports. Other ships near the scene quickly closed in.

"I ran to the family cottage and related what I had witnessed to my mother, brother and sister. They listened with disbelief and my mother said, It would have been a ship with black smoke coming out of the funnel. The next morning wreckage was washed ashore at the beach and a story was being told in the village of a large ship being sunk. It was only then that I was believed.

"In the early 1960s I was involved in the production of Buccaneer MK1 aircraft for the Fleet Air Arm. I was part of a team carrying out deck landing and take-off trials in the English Channel. I met up with a chief Petty Officer who was a survivor of *Dasher*. He vividly described to me how as a Fleet Air Arm mechanic he had been 'stood down' and had just left the hangar area when the explosion occurred. He considered himself to be very fortunate as if he had been in the hangar area one minute longer he would most certainly have perished."

# William John McCrae

Retired Artificer Sergeant Major

"I was born on the island of Arran and as a teenager I decided to make a career for myself in H M Forces. Although many years have passed, I still remember very vividly one particular Saturday afternoon on the island. I was gathering firewood and I was being helped by my brother, Duncan and a friend, Jimmy Campbell. Jimmy and his family were evacuees from war torn Glasgow.

"As the three of us emerged from a wood, which was halfway between Corrie and Sannox, we noticed smoke out to sea. It was very black smoke. I could make out the outline of a ship which was going up at the bow and the sailors were jumping overboard.

"We were in a direct line from the ship and it was a very clear day. Everything that was happening seemed to be so close to us. As we were looking at the burning ship, there were planes flying overhead.

"As we stood watching, the ship started to go down at the stern. Just then Mr Laughlin Milne, a local artist came over to us and hurried us away from our vantage point. His intentions were kind as he was trying to spare us possible unpleasant scenes. He said to us that it was probably an exercise.

"I made enquiries on the island about the 'incident'. However nobody seemed to want to discuss the subject. It was not until 1993 when a plaque was being unveiled in Ardrossan that I became aware of the large loss of life from the sea disaster that I had witnessed with my brother and Jimmy Campbell."

## Local lady

Name and address withheld by request

"My husband was a police officer stationed in Ardrossan. The first we knew of the disaster was when the survivors were being brought ashore. Many of them were badly burned.

"That night and for the next few days, the Women's Voluntary Service worked very hard collecting clothes for the survivors.

"The task of cleaning the badly burned bodies was carried out by Lawrie McLean, the local undertaker from Glasgow Street. He was assisted by my husband and his fellow officers who were accustomed to dealing with bodies recovered from the local harbour. The cleaning of the bodies was carried out in the makeshift mortuary in Harbour Street.

"A few days later, I was present as the large funeral procession marched slowly up the main street of Ardrossan. Later that day, I spoke to a family of relatives of one of the deceased. They showed me his photograph. He was only a boy and he had red hair. It was all very very sad.

"The so-called peace which we now have was at great cost."

## Mrs Elizabeth Schlund

Lochranza, Isle of Arran

"In 1943 I was a coding officer in the WRNS attached to Cypher Communication, Greenock. On Saturday 27th March 1943 I was on leave in Arran and cycling along the Corrie to Brodick road. I heard a fearful explosion. Looking seaward I saw an aircraft carrier which was obviously in terrible trouble. Black smoke was everywhere and I realised that I was witnessing a horrible tragedy.

"On returning to duty in Greenock, I was informed, Something terrible had happened which could not be discussed as I had not been on duty at the time.

"I asked if it was about the aircraft carrier blowing up, because if it was, I had actually seen it happen. They were all very surprised."

Dasher *casualties being taken ashore at Greenock*

## Captain L A K Boswell DSO

Captain Boswell was the captain who went down with his ship and survived. Having given the order, Abandon Ship! the captain made his way to the deck. The ship was now almost vertical. The captain reported that he slipped down the very steep deck and caught his foot on a stanchion, from which he was unable to free himself.

The aircraft carrier was now going under. The floating survivors took one last look and those in the water tried to get away as far as possible for fear of being pulled under.

Like the remainder of the crew still aboard the ship, the captain was fighting for his life. However his foot remained jammed.

As the aircraft carrier slipped under the cold waters of the Clyde estuary, almost unbelievably the ship created no 'pull'. The crew struggling in the water were safe, or so they thought.

As *Dasher* made her way down, Captain Boswell's foot became free and he shot to the surface. He was picked up from the water by the crew of the radar training ship *Isle of Sark*. A truly amazing escape. Understandably because of this experience he was not in a fit state of health to attend the Board of Enquiry into the incident.

Predictably this story circulated over the years of the captain who went down with his ship and survived. One version holds that it was when the ship vibrated on the sea bed, this had the effect of loosening the trapped captain's foot. This does seem unlikely. *Dasher* lies to this day at a depth of 170 metres and the likelihood of descending to this depth before surfacing and still surviving must be remote. Another report stated that it was Captain Boswell's coat that had been caught. However Commander Lane told his family that the captain had informed him at Ardrossan, "My foot was caught in a stanchion and I could not free it."

## Lt Commander James McGloin

James McGloin was involved in special duties in the Met office aboard *Dasher* with Sub Lt Langley. James McGloin explained that he avoided catastrophe by sheer coincidence.

"Sub Lt Langley was kind enough to release me to attend an Admiralty interview for a commission and I departed *Dasher* at very short notice on 26th March 1943, the evening before the explosion."

He had been friendly with the Surgeon Commander and the Commander Flying and also with Bill, the Sick Bay 'Tiffy' whose wife he had met in Liverpool. These three friends perished.

"Both Mrs Langley and Bill's wife wrote to me. There was nothing I could tell Mrs Langley about the disaster. However Bill's wife asked me if I thought Bill would approve of her remarrying. Luckily I could tell her that Bill and I had in fact discussed this very subject and Bill had said, If anything happens to me I hope that my wife will marry again."

Ordinary Seaman James McGloin later rose to the rank of Lt Commander. We can imagine his astonishment when he returned from his commission interview and was greeted at Glasgow Central Station by shipmates who were 'glad to see that he had survived'. He was innocently returning to the ship that was now no more.

James McGloin's pay book is stamped BEDDING RETURNED on 26th March—two blankets and one pillow case returned to stores aboard *Dasher*

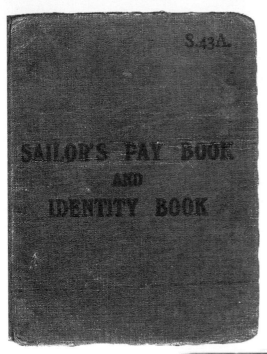

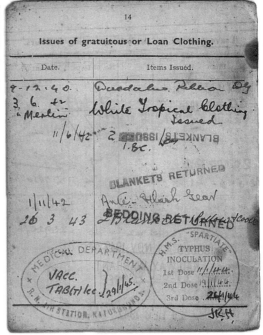

## Robert Brown

Resident of Saltcoats

My father served in the First World Was as a photographer in the Royal Flying Corps. Most of his service was spent in France.

Then from 1919 till 1960 he managed his own successful photographic studio. During the Second World War, he was involved in a great deal of photographic work for the Royal Navy at HMS *Fortitude* (Ardrossan). One of his duties was to photograph the survivors from HMS *Dasher*. The reason for this was the fear that a German might have slipped ashore, posing as a survivor.

*Page 80. Ordinary Seaman James McGloin. (Inset) James McGloin (1994)*
*Page 81. His paybook and identity book is dated 26th March 1943. Two blankets and one pillow case returned to stores aboard* Dasher

CHAPTER 4

# MISSING ON WAR SERVICE

Officer casualties

| | |
|---|---|
| Allan, William Lothian | Ty Act Lt Cdr (E) RNR |
| Banister, Maurice James | Ty Sub Lt (A) RNVR |
| Barker, Frank Ernest Joseph | Ty Sub-Lt (E) RNVR |
| Buxton, Trevor Victor | Ty Act Sub-Lt (E) RNVR |
| Cameron, Angus | Ty Act Sub-Lt (E) RNVR |
| Cuthbert, John Nicholas | Schoolmaster RN |
| Davies, Kenneth William | Lieutenant RNR |
| Haughie, William Pratt | Ty Act Sub-Lt (E) RNVR |
| Havers, Patrick Howard | Lt Cdr RN |
| Hughes, John | Ty Lt RN |
| Hutchinson, Robert | Ty Act Sub-Lt (E), RNVR |
| Johnston, Owen Temple | Sub-Lt RN |
| Langley, John Robert | Ty Sub-Lt, RNVR |
| Lincoln, Albert Harry | Ty Lt (E) RNVR |
| Lockwood, William Keith | Ty Sub-Lt (A) RNVR |
| McFarlane, John Lyle | Ty Act Sub-Lt (E) RNVR |

Monks, Newton Lee Ponting    Ty Pay Sub-Lt RNR
Moore, Thomas J A            Ty Sub-Lt (E) RNR
Paden, Richard               Ty Sub-Lt (A) RNVR
Price, Fleetwood Elwin        Ty Lt RNR
Scotchmoor, John William     Ty Lt Cdr (E) RNR
Stallard-Penoyre,
    Ralph Carnac Baker       Lieutenant RN
Storey, Thomas Pollard, DSC  Ty Surg Lt RNVR
Swan, William Arthur         Ty Act Sub-Lt (E) RNVR
Tetlow, Frank                Ty Act Sub-Lt (E) RNVR
Walker, John Russel          Ty Sub-Lt (A) RNVR
Wrathall, John Sandford      Ty Act Lt RNVR

## Missing Presumed Killed

| | | |
|---|---|---|
| Abrahams, Cyril J | Air Mechanic 2nd Class | FAA/FX.83180 |
| Acott, Frank A G | Ordinary Seaman | C/JX.376489 |
| Allan, William F | Steward | D/LX.26746 |
| Allen, Arthur E | Telegraphist | C/JX.149039 |
| Allen, Bernard | Able Seaman | C/JX.301148 |
| Almond, Eric | Ordinary Seaman | P/JX.372307 |
| Anderson, Alexander | Ordinary Seaman | C/JX.372884 |
| Anderson, George S | Air Mechanic 2nd Class | FAA/FX.81026 |
| Anstruther, David R | Ordinary Seaman | D/JX.348819 |
| Arslett, Frederick J | Air Mechanic (E) 1st Class | FAA/SFX.2476 |
| Atherton, Charles E | Able Seaman | C/JX.260436 |
| Ayers, Stanley | Carpenter's Mate | T.124.X |
| Bailey, John W | Signalman | C/JX.309419 |
| Baker, Valentine J | Yeoman Signals (Ty) R.F.R. | C/J.107758 |
| Barnes, William | Able Seaman | C/JX.238822 |
| Bartley, Ernest S | Ordinary Telegraphist | C/JX.341560 |
| Barwise, John H | Able Seaman | C/JX.259141 |
| Batchelor, Jack H | Air Mechanic (L) 1st Class | FAA/SFX.2517 |
| Baylis, Michael V | Signalman | C/JX.344709 |
| Bennett, Jack D | Ordinary Seaman | C/JX.332202 |
| Bevin, Gordon A | Ordinary Coder | C/JX.344942 |

| | | |
|---|---|---|
| Bingham, George C | Able Seaman | C/JX.319257 |
| Bland, Ivan H | Ordinary Seaman | C/JX.355221 |
| Bloomfield, Leonard W | Leading Radio Mechanic (AW) | FAA/FX.100747 |
| Boag-Jones, Dennis P | Air Mechanic (A) 1st Class | FAA/FX.82212 |
| Bond, Douglas A | Ordinary Signalman | C/JX.344711 |
| Botton, Norman D | Leading Supply Assistant (Ty) | C/MX.69527 |
| Bottril, Cuthbert L | Able Seaman | C/JX.303407 |
| Bowles, George B | Scullion | T.124.X |
| Bowman, Horace E | Leading Radio Mechanic(AW) | FAA/FX.82231 |
| Boyle, Francis | Able Seaman | C/JX.312325 |
| Bramhall, Edward L | Diesel Greaser | T.124.X |
| Bramwell, Reginald R | Ordinary Seaman | C/JX.351198 |
| Brandreth, James | Assistant Cook | T.124.X |
| Bretherton, Thomas F | Able Seaman | C/SSX.36069 |
| Brett, Dennis G | Air Mechanic (O) 1st Class | FAA/SFX.1499 |
| Brown, Alexander M | Ordinary Seaman | C/JX.376796 |
| Brown,Clifford T B | Leading Seaman (Ty) | C/JX.151184 |
| Brown, John H | Air Fitter (O) | FAA/FX.77765 |
| Brown, Robert B | Able Seaman | P/JX.266654 |
| Bryant, Daniel W | Leading Telegraphist.RNV(W)R | C/WRX.139 |
| Burls, Frank C | Able Seaman | C/JX.190291 |
| Burness, Albert E | Acting Able Seaman | C/SSX.34144 |
| Bursey, Graham | Able Seaman | C/JX.246665 |
| Bush, John R | Leading Seaman (Ty) | C/JX.145580 |
| Buswell, Peter E V | Air Mechanic (A) 1st Class | FAA/FX,83909 |
| Butler William A | Able Seaman | C/JX.277273 |
| Butterfield, Joseph N | Able Seaman | C/JX.279269 |
| Byrne, David E | Able Seaman | C/JX.225994 |
| Caldow, Robert | Ordinary Seaman | C/JX.352223 |
| Campbell, John C | Acting Able Seaman | C/JX.262397 |
| Candlish, William | Able Seaman | C/JX.237543 |
| Capstick, Joseph A | Chief Petty Officer Telegr. | C/J.46054 |
| Carrat, Walter | Able Seaman | C/JX.199849 |
| Carter, Harold O | Yeoman of Signals Ty. | C/SSX.17317 |
| Casson, William E A | Actign Able Seaman | C/JX.197543 |
| Castle, Rex | Assistant Steward | D/LX.29115 |

| | | |
|---|---|---|
| Chaplin, George W B | Chief Petty Officer A F (E) | FAA/F.55010 |
| Chappel, Ronald A | Assistant Steward | T.124.X |
| Clark, Arthur S | Air Mechanic (E) 2nd Class | FAA/FX.86308 |
| Clark, William E | Leading Seaman Ty. | C/JX.160256 |
| Clauson, William D | Able Seaman | C/SSX.23479 |
| Clayton, James | Leading Seaman Ty. | C/JX.142952 |
| Clements, Kenneth G | Leading Steward | T.124.X |
| Cluett, William G | Air Mechanic (O) 1st Class | FAA/FX.86307 |
| Cockerell, Leslie H | Acting Able Seaman | C/JX.248813 |
| Comber, Alfred J | Able Seaman | P/J.94507 |
| Combstock, Frederick J | Ordinary Seaman | D/JX.347470 |
| Congdon, Noel C E | Ordinary Seaman | P/JX.357886 |
| Cooley, Reginald D | Leading Radio Mechanic (AW) | FAA/FX.87765 |
| Corral, Noel L | Able Seaman | C/JX.319290 |
| Coulson, George V T | Able Seaman | C/JX.148891 |
| Cox, Frederick J | Assistant Steward | T.124.X |
| Crooks, Ivor E | Ordinary Seaman | C/JX.379344 |
| Cunningham, Albert | Able Seaman RNVR | C/LDX.2494 |
| Dando, Edwin J | Acting Leading Airman (Ty) | FAA/SFX.2864 |
| Davis, Stanley | Leading Seaman Ty. | C/JX.225276 |
| Davison, Edward H | Able Seaman | C/JX.168959 |
| Dawson, Albert J B | Leading Air Mechanic (L) | FAA/SFX.628 |
| Day, Frederick G W | Able Seaman RNVR | C/LDX.5093 |
| Devlin, John | Carpenter's Mate | T.124X. |
| Dickson, William | Leading Steward | T.124.X |
| Diggins, John H | Able Seaman | C/JX.193568 |
| Donoghue, Sydney T | Able Seaman | C/JX.224628 |
| Dowd, Thomas A | Petty Officer | C/JX.147634 |
| Edwards, Augustus | Able Seaman | C/JX.201321 |
| Fahey, John T | Acting Able Seaman | P/JX.321159 |
| Falla, Lesley L | Ordinary Telegraphist | C/JX.271799 |
| Farley, William G | Assistant Cook | T.124.X |
| Farthing, Ronald A | Assistant Cook | T.124.X |
| Ferneyhough, Wilfred | Able Seaman | C/JX.189663 |
| Fisher, Albert S | Electrical Artificer | C/SR.8276 |
| Fitzgerald, Anthony | Able Seaman | C/JX.220913 |

| | | |
|---|---|---|
| Flanagan, Dennis | Diesel Greaser | T.124.X |
| Flower, Kenneth H | Acting Petty Officer AM. (O) | FAA/FX.77086 |
| Fox, George E | Air Mechanic (A) 1st Class | FAA/FX.79161 |
| French, William E P | Stoker 1st Class | C/KX.105295 |
| Fulker, Henry C | Air Mechanic (E) | FAA/FX.92524 |
| Furrell, Patrick R | Supply Petty Officer | C/MX.52485 |
| Gamble, John M | Leading Radio Mechanic (AR) | FAA/FX.88200 |
| Gibson, John A | Carpenter's Mate | T.124.X |
| Gibson, Roy | Acting Able Seaman | C/JX.316841 |
| Gilbert, James W | Ordinary Seaman | C/JX.317966 |
| Gilroy, James | Able Seaman | C/JX.315140 |
| Goswell, Richard F | RPO (DNA SC 8222/43) | C/M.40032 |
| Gray, Archibald | Boatswain | T.124.X |
| Griffin, Bertie W | Able Seaman | P/JX.316118 |
| Griffiths, Charles W | Diesel Greaser | T.124.X |
| Griffiths, William R | Air Fitter (E) | FAA/SFX.2042 |
| Gunner, Frederick J | Able Seaman | C/JX.195146 |
| Habgood, George A | Butcher 1st Class | T.124.X |
| Hambrook, Robert F | Chief Yeoman of Signals | C/J.110579 |
| Hampton, Thom F | Able Seaman | W/SSX.13594 |
| Handley, Donald C | Leading Radio Mechanic (AR) | FAA/JX.357091 |
| Handley, John G | Acting Leading Air Mechanic (E) | FAA/SFX.264 |
| Handy, Ernest H | Petty Officer | C/JX.134868 |
| Harrop, Thomas | Air Fitter (E) | FAA/FX.83023 |
| Hart, Henry | Donkeyman | T.124.X |
| Hartill, Horace | Naval Airman 2nd Class | FAA/FX.93960 |
| Harvey, Clayton W A | Able Seaman | C/JX.316615 |
| Harvey, William J | Able Seaman | C/JX.279344 |
| Haskayne, James A | Leading Radio Mechanic (AW) | FAA/FX.82981 |
| Hicks, Joseph | Air Mechanic (E) 1st Class | FAA/FX.84551 |
| Hill, James O T | Able Seaman | C/JX.316502 |
| Hill, Joseph | Ship's Cook | T.124.X |
| Hind, Bert J | Air Mechanic (O) 1st Class | FAA/FX.92579 |
| Hobbs, Joseph F | Able Seaman | C/JX.278289 |
| Hodkinson, Percy C | Telegraphist | C/JX.178427 |
| Hodkinson, Peter | Leading Radio Mechanic | P/MX.102049 |

| | | |
|---|---|---|
| Horne, John R | Sick Berth Attendant | C/MX.85545 |
| Horne, Sylvester R A J | Air Mechanic (E) 1st Class | FAA/FX.83836 |
| Howse, Leslie G T | Photographer (A) | FAA/MX.101858 |
| Hoyle, Laurence | Leading Air Fitter (E) | FAA/SFX.2913 |
| Humphreys, Albert | Leading Seaman Ty | C/JX.127052 |
| Hurst, Frederick M | Ship's Cook | T.124.X |
| Inglesfield, Joseph | Able Seaman | C/JX.333162 |
| Ingram, Dennis A | Assistant Steward | T.124.X |
| Irvine, George B | Supply Assistant | P/MX.82797 |
| Jackson, Henry R | Leading Airman Ty | FAA/FX.87319 |
| Jackson, Leonard | Acting Able Seaman | C/JX.315182 |
| Jackson, Stephen | Baker 1st Class | T.124.X |
| Jeffrey, Andrew | Diesel Greaser | T.124.X |
| Jennings, Nelson P | Able Seaman | C/LDX.4789 |
| Johnson, Harold W | Ordinary Signalman | C/JX.298702 |
| Joy, Edwin G | Air Mechanic(A) 1st Class | FAA/FX.84427 |
| Kemp, Oscar C | Petty Officer | C/JX.130904 |
| Kenah, John E | Able Seaman | C/JX.279071 |
| Kennedy, William | Able Seaman | C/JX.182786 |
| Keverne, Richard H J | Acting Petty Officer | |
| | Air Mechanic | (O)FAA/FX.77087 |
| Kilburn, William | Chief Steward 1st Class | T.124.X |
| Kilpatrick, Samuel J | Able Seaman | P/JX.306997 |
| Knowles, Frank | Able Seaman | C/JX.319685 |
| Kyle, Charles Mc | Able Seaman | C/JX.289245 |
| Langston, Enos J | Air Mechanic (E) 1st Class | FAA/FX.82213 |
| Levick, Roy E | Acting Leading Air Mechanic (E) | FAA/FX.76058 |
| Lewis, Alan W G | Assistant Steward | T.124.X |
| Lightwing, James A | Ordinary Seaman | C/JX.374404 |
| Linfield, William S L | Able Seaman | C/JX.247986 |
| Loade, William | Steward | D/LX.26017 |
| Lonsdale, Cyril | Air Mechanic (O) 2nd Class | FAA/FX.94533 |
| Luffingham, Arthur | Able Seaman | C/SSX.15239 |
| Lumby, Arthur | Leading Radio Mechanic (AW) | FAA/FX.87283 |
| MacAulay, Hugh | Ordinary Seaman | C/JX.316449 |
| McCann, Joseph | Air Mechanic (E) 1st Class | FAA/SFX.906 |

| | | |
|---|---|---|
| McCarthy, Daniel | Able Seaman | C/JX.201329 |
| McCarthy, Victor D | Able Seaman | C/JX.195151 |
| McCracken, Peter W | Naval Airman 2nd Class | FAA/FX.90055 |
| McLean, Walter | Ordinary Seaman | C/JX.352453 |
| McLellan, John | Air Mechanic 2nd Class (Other) | FAA/FX.84560 |
| McMurray, John P | Naval Airman 2nd Class | FAA/FX.101282 |
| McSwain, James M | Leading Seaman | D/J.27914 |
| Mahon, James T | Able Seaman | C/JX.173315 |
| Mahon, William | Air Mechanic (O) 1st Class | FAA/FX.84092 |
| Mahoney, Edward J | Air Mechanic (L) 1st Class | FAA/SFX.2430 |
| Maidment, Walter J | Diesel Greaser | T.124.X |
| Mainland, James S | Acting Leading Air Mechanic (L) | FAA/SFX.612 |
| Marson, William | Able Seaman | C/JX.316912 |
| Marston, Henry C | Able Seaman | C/JX.300111 |
| Mason, Henry S | Ordinary Telegraphist | C/JX.250509 |
| Mason, William C | Leading Supply Assistant (Ty) | C/MX.84090 |
| Maxted, Jack | Assistant Cook | T.124.X |
| Maxwell, Robert | Air Mechanic (A) 1st Class | FAA/FX.80667 |
| Milsted, William H | Ordinary Seaman | C/JX.331451 |
| Mitchell, David J | Leading Supply Assistant (Ty) | C/MX.94654 |
| Mollett, Henry G | Ordinary Seaman | C/JX.353724 |
| Moody, George E | Leading Seaman (Ty) | C/JX.133401 |
| Moody, Joseph H | Acting Leading Airman (Ty) | FAA/FX.89609 |
| Moore, John R | Air Mechanic 2nd Class | FAA/SR.317 |
| Morgan, Frederick A | Able Seaman | C/JX.137744 |
| Morgan, John J | Leading Seaman | P/JX.186173 |
| Mosey, Walter | Able Seaman | C/SSX.25471 |
| Moss, Alexander M | Saloon Steward | T.124.X |
| Mouland, John H L | Acting Leading Air Mechanic (E) | FAA/SFX.1242 |
| Mudd, Horace H | Acting Able Seaman | P/JX.315913 |
| Mullins, James | Air Mechanic 2nd Class | FAA/FX.89500 |
| Murton, Norman | Sick Berth Petty Officer (Ty) | C/MX.49288 |
| Neighbour, Thomas H | Able Seaman | C/JX.299146 |
| Nethercott, Henry E | Steward | D/LX.26845 |
| Nichol, Wilfred J | Carpenter's Mate | T.124.X |
| Nicholson, Albert J | Able Seaman | C/JX.240864 |

| | | |
|---|---|---|
| Norman, Frank | Air Mechanic (A) 1st Class | FAA/SFX.2593 |
| Norton, John B | Signalman | C/JX.148936 |
| Nunn, Arthur D | Air Mechanic (E) 1st Class | FAA/FX.83693 |
| Oakman, Stanley | Ordinary Seaman | C/JX.315571 |
| O'Brien, Arnold | Ordinary Seaman | C/JX.353051 |
| O'Connnor, Francis J | Able Seaman | C/JX.279101 |
| O'Donnel, John | Cleaner | T.124.X |
| O'Malley, Charles E | Cleaner | T.124.X |
| O'Neil, John | Fireman | T.124.X |
| Oxford, William A | Fireman | T.124.X |
| Paice, Reginal E | Air Mechanic (O) 2nd Class | FAA/FX.94546 |
| Parkinson, Donald | Air Mechanic (L) 1st Class | FAA/SFX.2616 |
| Paterson, James R | Assistant Baker | T.124.X |
| Paxton, George W | Leading Air Fitter (A) | FAA/FX.83231 |
| Peet, Joseph D O | Air Fitter (O) | FAA/FX.82416 |
| Pell, Fred | Leading Airman (Ty) | FAA/JX.193497 |
| Petty, Charles J | Able Seaman | C/JX.278463 |
| Phillibrown, Harry C | Ordinary Seaman | C/JX.374889 |
| Pigden, Charles F | Ordinary Seaman | C/JX.374891 |
| Pitman, Peter E V | 1st Writer | T.124.X |
| Pile, Stephen G | Petty Officer | C/J.101696 |
| Plant, Percy H | Able Seaman | C/JX.283544 |
| Playford, Cyril E | Able Seaman | C/JX.160947 |
| Potter, Lawrence | Assistant Steward | T.124.X |
| Price, Percy D | Stoker 1st Class | C/KX.90532 |
| Rayward, Clifford | Air Mechanic (O) 1st Class | FAA/JX.231349 |
| Reed, Robert | Ordinary Seaman | C/JX.352493 |
| Reeves, John | Petty Officer Air Fitter (O) | FAA/FX.80136 |
| Reid, Allan | Cleaner | T.124.X |
| Richardson, George T | Petty Officer Air Fitter (O) | FAA/FX.79940 |
| Richardson, Harry | Able Seaman | C/JX.171624 |
| Richardson, William | Storekeeper 1st Class | T.124.X |
| Richer, Jack | Able Seaman | D/J.59908 |
| Rix, Richard D | Ordinary Seaman | C/JX.353084 |
| Roberts, Dennis | Mechanic | T.124.X |
| Roberts, Geoffrey | Air Fitter (A) | FAA/FX.86050 |

| | | |
|---|---|---|
| Roberts, Peter | Leading Telegraphist | C/JX.143601 |
| Robinson, William J | Saloon Steward | T.124.X |
| Robson, James | Acting Able Seaman | C/JX.314025 |
| Rockcliff, John | Ordinary Seaman | C/JX.354227 |
| Rodway, Harry | Air Mechanic (O) 2nd Class | FAA/FX.94665 |
| Rogerson, Norman J | Air Mechanic (E) 1st Class | FAA/FX.82785 |
| Rolph, Alfred J | Stoker 1st Class | C/KX.104771 |
| Ross, Henry | Air Mechanic (A) 1st Class | FAA/FX.83784 |
| Ross, Henry | Painter | T.124.X |
| Routley, Harold G | Acting Petty Officer Air Mechanic (E) | FAA/FX.76574 |
| | | |
| Salmon, John T | Leading Steward (Ty) | D/LX.24940 |
| Salter, Samuel J | Air Mechanic (E) 1st Class | FAA/FX.83109 |
| Scanlon, Thomas | Able Seaman | C/JX.237014 |
| Schooling, Joseph R | Acting Leading Air Mechanic (L) | FAA/FX.76644 |
| Scott, William H | Able Seaman | C/JX.172434 |
| Scragg, Francis H | Acting Air Artificer 4th Class | FAA/FX.75576 |
| Seward, Leslie A | Able Seaman | C/JX.161731 |
| Sharpe, William C | Able Seaman | C/JX.199851 |
| Sheldon, Horace V | Sick Berth Attendent | C/MX.94630 |
| Sheppard, John A | Ordinary Seaman | C/JX.374470 |
| Shirley, Edward W | Leading Air Fitter (L) | FAA/FX.75535 |
| Shuttleworth, George W | Air Mechanic (A) 1st Class | FAA/SFX.1037 |
| Simmonds, Arthur S | Air Mechanic (L) 1st Class | FAA/FX.80985 |
| Simpson, Dennis W | Air Mechanic (A) 1st Class | FAA/FX.84460 |
| Skinner, Leslie R | Leading Telegraphist | C/SSX.16331 |
| Slade, John | Diesel Greaser | T.124.X |
| Smith, Ernest F | Photographer (A) | FAA/MX.93131 |
| Smith, Leslie D | Ordnance Artificer 4th Class | C/MX.76076 |
| Sneddon, William B | Air Mechanic (L) 1st Class | FAA/FX.79517 |
| Snell, Ivan | Air Mechanic (O) 1st Class | FAA/SFX.2335 |
| Spence, Alexander P M | Able Seaman | C/SSX.21966 |
| Spiers, William A | Signalman | C/JX.309405 |
| Sporton, Albert V H | Ordinary Seaman | P/JX.324724 |
| Spratt, Rodney N | Able Seaman | C/JX.199797 |
| Stamp, John G | Petty Officer RNVR | C/TD/X.909 |

| | | |
|---|---|---|
| Stanton, Roy L | Able Seaman | P/JX.323583 |
| Stead, Wilfred | Leading Radio Mechanic (AR) | FAA/FX.88236 |
| Stockford, Albert J | Air Mechanic (O) 2nd Class | FAA/FX.85689 |
| Sullivan, Thomas | Electrical Artificer 2nd Class | C/MX.46283 |
| Sweetnam, Cuthbert B | Supply Assistant | D/MX.107019 |
| Tallack, Richard J | Air Artificer 4th Class | FAA/SFX.344 |
| Taylor, Cyril G | Ordinary Seaman | C/JX.327124 |
| Taylor, Frederick J | Greaser | T.124.X |
| Tennant, Herbert W | Assistant Storekeeper | T.124.X |
| Terrey, Cyril J | Petty Officer Telegraphist | C/JX.134049 |
| Thistle, Cyril R | Able Seaman | C/JX.315756 |
| Thompson, James | Able Seaman | C/SSX.18878 |
| Thomson, Alexander M A | Naval Airman 2nd Class | FAA/FX.98233 |
| Thornhill, Raymond | Able Seaman | C/JX.318466 |
| Tickner, William T | Acting Radio Petty Officer (Ty) | C/J.109099 |
| Timmis, Robert | Able Seaman | C/SSX.24437 |
| Tinto, Leslie G | Scullion | T.124.X |
| Tomblin, William J R | Coder | C/JX.293104 |
| Tordoff, Dennis A | Carpenter's Mate | T.124.X |
| Tosh, William | Assistant Steward | T.124.X |
| Travis, William | Storekeeper | T.124.X |
| Turner, Eric R | Air Mechanic (O) 2nd Class | FAA/FX.94452 |
| Turner, Frank O | Leading Seaman | C/SSX.20187 |
| Varcoe, Jack | Assistant Steward | D/LX.26736 |
| Vaughan, George | Assistant Cook | T.124.X |
| Voice, Stanley C | Leading Air Fitter (A) | FAA/FX.81775 |
| Wain, George W | Leading Air Mechanic (O) | FAA/SFX.144 |
| Walker, John C | Able Seaman | C/JX.169472 |
| Walsh, Thomas | Assistant Steward | T.124.X |
| Webb, Joseph H | Naval Airman 2nd Class | FAA/FX.94804 |
| Whittington, Richard A | Able Seaman | C/JX.173033 |
| Williams, Dennis R | Air Mechanic (O) 1st Class | FAA/FX.84125 |
| Williams, Robert | Air Mechanic (E) 1st Class | FAA/FX.90025 |
| Willis, Howard | Air Mechanic (O) 2nd Class | FAA/FX.94483 |
| Wood, George | Fireman | T.124.X |
| Woodward, Claude | Air Mechanic (O) 1st Class | FAA/FX.81670 |

| | | |
|---|---|---|
| Woolley, Henry G | Chief Petty Officer | C/J.105610 |
| Worsdell, Albert C | Ordinary Seaman | P/JX.345517 |
| Yates, Thomas | Able Seaman | C/JX.168689 |
| Young, Albert J | Petty Officer Airman | FAA/F.55142 |
| Young, Cecil A | Able Seaman | C/JX.316666 |

## N.A.A.F.I.

Missing Presumed Killed

| | |
|---|---|
| Cowen, David | Canteen Manager |
| Shearer, James D | Canteen Assistant |
| Webb, Victor | Leading Canteen Assistant |

## Royal Air Force Personnel

| | | |
|---|---|---|
| Grieve, Alexander | Flight Sergeant | 564019 |

Missing Presumed Killed

| | | |
|---|---|---|
| Leonard, Roger | Sergeant | 523319 |
| Parks, Stanley Muirson | Corporal | 533572 |

CHAPTER 5

# THE INQUIRY INTO THE LOSS OF

# HMS *DASHER*

After suffering the loss of their ship, with many of their shipmates still on board, witnessing the deaths of scores of the crew to the searing flames in the water, three days later on Tuesday 30th March twenty six of the survivors were taken out in open boat to *Dasher's* sister ship HMS *Archer*.

Here the Board of Enquiry would start at 09.30 that morning into the cause or causes of Saturday's tragic loss of life. HMS *Archer* was at anchor at the Tail o' the Bank, Greenock.

As the open boat made its way to the aircraft carrier Archer, the twenty six crew of *Dasher* must have suffered further trauma. They were looking up at an almost identical ship to the one that had sunk three days previously. The enquiry commenced that Tuesday morning and concluded the following day. It was restricted to naval personnel only. Local civilian witnesses were not invited.

The minutes of the Board of Enquiry make interesting reading. Extending to sixty four pages, they appear to include all witnesses called and questions asked. In addition to the twenty six survivors from the crew of *Dasher*, some witnesses from nearby naval vessels were also in attendance and were called to give evidence. Commanding officers from HMS *Isle of Sark*, from *La Capricieuse* and from *Dasher*'s own motor launch were called.

Unfortunately the master of *Dasher*, Captain L A K Boswell was too ill to attend.

The Board of Enquiry comprised five men of Captain or Commander rank, including the captain of the host vessel and *Dasher*'s sister ship, HMS *Archer*. During the course of the enquiry the board visited the hangar, petrol control room, petrol stowage compartment, shaft tunnel, engine room and depth charge magazine of HMS *Archer*, presumably to familiarise themselves with the layout of the doomed ship. Plans for HMS *Biter* (another sister ship) are also recorded as having been made available to members of the board.

A perusal of the questioning recorded in the minutes of the two day investigation gives an insight into the thinking of the board. Was the explosion internal or had *Dasher* been hit from outside? What was she loaded with? What were the procedures for fuel and explosives maintenance? Were procedures carried out and was there any smoking below decks?

The most senior surviving officer from the crew of *Dasher* who was present was Commander E W E Lane. He was called first to give evidence. As with all witnesses he was placed under oath, or in naval parlance he was cautioned in accordance with KRAI, Article 488, paragraph 9.

"Will you please explain briefly," asked president of the Board of Enquiry, Captain G Grantham of HMS *Indomitable,* "what you know of the circumstances of this case, to the best of your ability?"

Commander Lane's reply is full and worth quoting at length.

The ship left Lamlash shortly after 11 o'clock on Saturday morning and proceeded to sea for flying exercises. She was operating east of Arran. Flying ceased about 16.30 and a course was shaped for Greenock. A signal was made asking for the

*HMS* Archer, Dasher's *sister ship—the Board of Inquiry was held on board three days after the disaster*

Gate at 18.00. Word had been passed by the captain over the loudspeakers that leave would be granted to one watch. At about 16.45 I went up on to the bridge to find out our expected time of arrival. I looked at the chart and on it was a copy of our signal asking for the Gate. I was about to write down what I was doing when the ship shuddered, aft, accompanied by a bang, not very loud. My immediate reaction was that there had been an explosion in the engine or boiler up-takes, as it was similar to previous explosions of that nature. I looked over the bridge and my first view was confirmation of this. Smoke and small black objects were travelling horizontally on the starboard side. I then saw very much more smoke than we had before, and further aft. The Officer of the Watch then said, "Crikey, look at that." "That" was the lift entire, perfectly horizontal, sailing away 50 feet above the flight deck. I then noticed considerable flames and smoke were rising from the lift opening, and the flight deck itself was buckled up to half the after length of the hangar. On the starboard side there were two burst places out of which flame and smoke were appearing.

There were volumes of smoke accompanied by large tongues of flame. I went down on to the flight deck and told the hands who were standing round to run hoses. The captain then called me from the bridge and asked me what had happened. I said I did not know but I would find out. The ship had taken a gradually increasing list to starboard and appeared down by the stern, but by the time the captain called me the ship had returned quickly upright but trimmed by the stern. I went down on to the first deck and made my way to the second deck by ladder outside the captain's cabin. I proceeded aft along the port alleyway. There were no lights, but smoke and debris were there and further aft the gangway was obstructed, by the galley and CPO's Mess, approximately 108 Station, ie above the engineroom, and about 80 feet forward of the petrol stowage. By this time the ship was still further down by the stern, smoke was very thick and there was the sound of rushing water and grinding metal from below and aft. I looked down a hatch outside the provision issue room, that is on 105 Station, and I could hear water pouring in. I saw about three feet of water on the third deck. This hatch gave me access to the engineroom aft and a recreation space forward. The ship seemed to be settled aft, and I made my way to the upper deck by the same route I had come. I looked in cabins and offices but they appeared to be empty to the port side. I endeavoured to get hands to swing out the boats. Carley floats etc were already being released from the walkways. Water was now coming over the upper deck, level with the forward end of the hangar. I crawled forward to the port lower boom and went over the side as the ship rapidly settled by the stern until she finally became vertical and went down.

Captain J M NcNair, captain of HMS *Isle of Sark* told the board that his ship had picked up thirty five survivors. "Survivors," he informed the inquiry when asked about petrol and oil on the water, "were covered in oil and difficult to get a hold of."

Sub Lieutenant E C D Holman was on *Dasher's* Motor Launch M L *528* at the time of the explosion. During flight practice this was normal procedure for a motor vessel to cruise around the carrier as a safety precaution should any aircraft ditch in the water.

About 16.40, we observed the after end of the flight deck appear to lift in the air, presumably after an explosion, followed shortly after by a bigger explosion and a lot of black smoke which appeared to shoot over the starboard side of the ship, after which the ship appeared to list over to starboard and to settle by the stern. At the time of the second explosion an object was seen to shoot out of the top of the flight deck. I understand it was the lift, and it landed in the water on the port side.

ML *528* had been about three cables away. He was asked if the shock of the explosion had been felt on his vessel. Sub Lieutenant Holman answered,

Only that we felt the concussion as if a heavy gun had been fired. There was no shock as from an underwater explosion. I questioned all members of my crew who were below at the time and asked them whether they had heard anything. Some had heard nothing at all and others had heard the explosion, but do not appear to have felt anything much in the way of a shudder in the ship itself.

Did he see any column of water, he was asked, or anything to indicate that an explosion had taken place outside the ship?

No, sir. We did not see any displacement of water at all or anything of that nature.

So was Sub Lieutenant Holman of the opinion that the explosion was internal?

Yes, sir, he replied. It certainly looked that way to us.

Corroborated by the evidence of others, the cause of the disaster could be looked for then, not in the unlikely presence and firing by an enemy destroyer or U-boat, but to the internal workings of the *Dasher* herself.

In the findings of the Board of Enquiry reproduced in full in the next chapter, in the recommendations made, in surviving correspondence and in the record of the particular witnesses called more than once to give evidence, it appears that *Dasher* contained the seeds of her own destruction.

Lieutenant Commander Wootton was recalled and subjected to a further thirty two questions on the engineroom, a shaft tunnel, the procedures for checking fuel tanks, no smoking procedures and such matters. He was recalled a second time and examined by the board about the petrol compartment, during the course of which it emerged that there was a known leakage from one of the tanks in the main petrol store. The rate of leakage was said by Commander Wootton to be "very slow—about one drip every five seconds."

It also emerged that as well as this 'very slow' leak from a petrol tank cock, that there was another potentially even more calamitous means by which highly imflamable fuel spirit could leak into uncontrolled areas. The enquiry board asked Commander Wootton when on one occasion the petrol stowage tanks were partially flooded and water was found leaking into the shaft tunnel, were the holes into the shaft tunnel properly plugged?

No, sir, replied Commander Wootton.

So they were, in fact, still open?

There was one hole about 1 inch in diameter. Actually it was a hole for an electric light cable but no wiring was run through it.

As the report of the board of inquiry draws attention to, and as future recriminatory correspondence between the British and American governments alludes to, the coversion of this vessel from a cargo ship to an aircraft carrier was an accident waiting to happen.

CHAPTER 6

# REPORT OF THE BOARD OF ENQUIRY

BOARD OF ENQUIRY HELD ON BOARD H.M.S. 'ARCHER' ON TUESDAY
AND WEDNESDAY, 30TH AND 31ST MARCH 1943 TO INVESTIGATE
INTO THE CIRCUMSTANCES ATTENDING

LOSS OF HMS 'DASHER' ON 27TH MARCH, 1943

SCHEDULE OF CONTENTS

Findings of the Board.
Memorandum convening the Board.
Schedule of Witnesses and No's of questions asked.
Minutes of proceedings.
Photographs and negatives of sinkings taken by
rating on board M.L. 528.
Original shorthand notes.

**SECRET**.

H.M.S. 'ARCHER'
    31st March, 1943

Sir,
In accordance with your Memorandum dated 28th March,
1943, directing us to enquire into the loss of HMS
'DASHER' on the 27th March, 1943, we have the honour to
submit the following report:-

2.       HMS 'DASHER' sank at approximately 1648A on 27th
      March in approximate position 205 degrees Cumbrae
      Island Light 5 miles. Commanding Officer and 148
      of her ship's company survived out of a total of
      527.

3.       <u>The following facts have been established</u>:-

(a)     Explosion was not due to any external cause.

(b)     It was a muffled rumbling report and not an
        instantaneous detonation.

(c)     It did not take place in the after 4" magazine;
        in the hangar; forward of the hangar in the
        engine room.

4.       <u>The explosion vented itself</u>:-

(a)     forward through the after bulkhead of the engine
        room low down.

(b)     upward through a large hatch just forward of the
        lift well.

(c)     up and out through the ship's side to starboard
        via the Fleet Air Arm messdeck.

(d)     presumably through the ship's bottom in one or
        more places.

5.      <u>The results of the explosion were</u>:-

(a)     Immediate failure of all light and power:
        emergency dynamo cut in for about 20 seconds
        only.

(b)     Lift, at flight deck level, blown high in the air
        and after end of flight deck damaged.

(c)     Violent fire at the end of hangar.

(d)     Fire in the engine room.

(e)     Rapid flooding of the ship extending from forward
        engine room bulkhead to the stern.

(f)     A list to starboard of not more than 10 degrees
        which rapidly disappeared as the ship settled
        quickly by the stern.

6.      <u>State of the ship was as follows</u>:-

(a)     Flying had just been completed and all aircraft
        except one struck down.

(b)     In the hangar were 6 Swordfish and 2 Hurricanes.
        Two Swordfish were being fuelled.

(c)     Petrol control room was open with Greaser in
        attendance.

(d)     Access hatch from Fleet Air Arm messdeck to flat
        outside petrol control room was open.

(e)     Hatch in same flat at top of access trunk to
        shaft tunnel may also have been open, as this was
        in regular use for hourly visits to Plummer
        Blocks.

(f)     A hole, 1" in diameter between the shaft tunnel
        and main petrol compartment was known to exist.

(g)     It is uncertain whether a slow drip from a valve
        on one of the starboard tanks had been made good.

(h)    Some of Fleet Air Arm personnel, who had been
       working on aircraft and dismissed from hangar,
       were on their messdeck. "No smoking" notices
       were permanently in place above hatch to petrol
       control room. No sentry was placed.

(i)    Hands had been working in after depth charge
       stowage which is immediately abaft the petrol
       compartment during the forenoon. 68 depth
       charges were still in this magazine.

7.    We are of the opinion that:-

(I)    The original explosion took place either in the
       after depth charge magazine or the main petrol
       stowage. These two compartments are adjacent to
       one another.

(II)   There is no evidence that the explosion occurred
       in the depth charge magazine beyond the fact that
       this is located in the region of the explosion.

(III)  There is no direct proof that the explosion
       started in the main petrol stowage. But evidence
       shows that there may have been an accumulation of
       petrol vapour in the main petrol compartment and
       that this could have been ignited by a man
       smoking in the shaft tunnel, or through someone
       dropping a cigarette end down from the Fleet Air
       Arm messdeck, to the petrol control compartment
       of below.
       It is pointed out that the lighting system is not
       up to magazine lighting specification, and that a
       fault on the system could have ignited petrol
       vapour when lights were switched on or off.

8.    We recommend that:-

(A)    Alterations detailed in Commander-in-Chief, Home
       Fleet's telegram T.O.O. 1339 of 15th February
       1943 should be applied to all escort carriers at
       the earliest opportunity.

(B)    Access to petrol control compartments should be
       trunked up to the deck of the hangar, as in
       'ARCHER' and in no case to a crewspace.

(C)    Until B is carried out in existing carriers, the
       trunk giving access to the forward end of the
       shaft tunnel should not be used.

(D)    The watertight door giving access from the engine
       room to the shaft tunnel should be permanently
       sealed, as had already been done in 'DASHER'.

(E)    The shaft tunnel should be fitted with a
       ventilating system.

(F)    All carriers to be supplied at the earliest
       possible moment with portable petrol detector
       gauges.

(G)    All carriers be instructed to carry out rigidly
       magazine and petrol regulations, and that all
       defects in petrol systems are to be reported to
       the Commanding Officer immediately they are
       discovered.

(H)    All carriers be instructed that life belts are to
       be worn when ships are exercising in local areas
       as well as at sea.

(I)    Calcium Flares should be withdrawn from carriers,
       but if carried should be stored in a watertight
       container.

9.     The behaviour and bearing of the Officers and
       ratings was exemplary throughout.  Petty Officer
       STAMP R.N.V.R., assisted many young ratings to
       safety, but he lost his life in so doing.  Petty
       Officer Telegraphist TERRY displayed a similar
       spirit and example and was also lost.

10.     Two small coasting vessels, the S.S. 'LITHIUM'
        and S.S. 'CRAGSMAN' gave valuable assistance in
        rescuing men from the sea, working close to the
        oil burning on the water.


We have the honour to be,
     Sir,
Your obedient Servants, (signed)

        Captain G. Grantham C.B. D.S.O. R.N.
        (President) H.M.S. 'INDOMITABLE'

        Captain J.I. Robertson R.N.
        H.M.S. 'ARCHER'

        Constructor Captain R.G. Holt R.N.
        Staff of Commander-in-Chief, Home Fleet

        Commander R. Cobb O.B.E. R.N.
        H.M.S. 'INDOMITABLE'

        Commander H.D. McMaster R.N.R.
        H.M.S. 'ARCHER'

CHAPTER 7

# THE SHORT CAREER OF THE *DASHER*

During the years of the World War II, the battle of the Atlantic was the longest and most decisive. Without the convoys and their precious cargo, Britain would almost certainly have been defeated.

The convoys came under constant attack from the dreaded U-boats and from long range aircraft, so air cover was essential. Flying boats offered some protection but even the Sunderlands' great range was not enough. Aircraft carriers were urgently required to cover the Atlantic Gap between twenty and forty degrees longitude. The strategy was that the aircraft carrier would sail in the middle of the convoy, keeping the U-boats at bay with her aircraft flying around.

On April 29th 1942, the Admiralty ordered six 'Fighter Carriers' under the lease-lend agreement. Under this arrangement America would supply ships already built and convert them to Royal Navy specifications for use during hostilities.

These six ships were the first true escort carriers based on the standard C3 mercantile hull. They were provided with a single aircraft lift connecting the flight deck and the hangar. The hangar occupies half the ship's length.

One of the ships to be converted was the *Rio de Janeiro*. Built by the Sun Shipbuilding Company , Hoboken, USA, it had been launched and was being fitted out as a cargo vessel to carry bananas. However she was to have a very different future to that envisaged by her designers and builders.

The *Rio de Janeiro* was taken from the Sun Shipbuilding Company to Tietsen and Laird, also of Hoboken. Here extensive work was carried out to convert her from a merchant ship to an aircraft carrier. A flight deck had to be fitted, a hangar and an aircraft lift for two squadrons of Hurricanes and one squadron of Swordfish. Accommodation was also fitted for a crew of five hundred and twenty seven.

The conversion was completed on July 1st 1942 and the ship was renamed HMS *Dasher*. Her specifications were as follows.

| | |
|---|---|
| Machinery | Sun Droxford Diesel (one shaft 8500 HP |
| Length Overall | 492 feet |
| Mean Draught | 25 feet |
| Flight Deck length | 410 feet |
| Speed | 16 knots |
| Armament | 3 x 4 HA |
| | 6 x 0.5" Colt |
| | 10 x 20mm Oerlikon |
| Aircraft compliment | Various |
| | 12 Sea Hurricanes OR |
| | 9 Sea Hurricanes and 6 Swordfish |
| Petrol Stowage | 75,000 gallons |
| Catapult | Fitted with an H2 accelerator. Suitable for American types of aircraft only. |

The former banana boat was now the Archer class escort carrier, *Dasher*. She was the fourth of these American built carriers, her true sisters being Avenger, Biter and Charger. Charger was retained in America under the command of the United States Navy and used to train Royal Navy aircrew, in American waters.

After the handover on July 1st, *Dasher* did not sail to Britain as planned. Because of persistent mechanical defects her departure was delayed for two months.

*Dasher's* chief engineer distrusted the design of the Sun Droxford engines and his low opinion appeared to be vindicated on many occasions. On the trial runs in the Brooklyn Navy Yard for example, the engines backfired frequently on starting up. On one occasion pieces flew out of the exhaust vents.

There was unpleasantness when a domestic boiler which contained no water was switched on and exploded. The two junior engineers responsible were personally run off the ship by the chief. They were reinstated two months later by the Ministry of Transport.

*Dasher* embarked four Swordfish in American waters, but two of them crashed off the bows during flying trials. The remaining two were reserved for the senior pilot to fly on the way to Britain.

HMS *Dasher* finally left Brooklyn Navy Yard in mid-August to await a convoy. Her captain over this period was Vice-Admiral R Bell-Davies, the famous naval aviator and VC of World War I. He had come back from retirement to active service as a Commander. He was now succeeded by Acting Captain CN Lentaignes DSO.

Two weeks later a convoy had assembled and *Dasher* was included. On departing, her engine misfired twice, then gave up. Eventually she made a full-speed dash through Long Island Sound and Cape Cod Canal and caught up with the convoy at Boston. She left for Halifax on August 30th, on her maiden voyage to the United Kingdom, with her senior pilot standing by to defend the convoy single handed. Happily the voyage was uneventful and *Dasher* berthed at Greenock on September 10th.

Like the other American built escort carriers, *Dasher* was in need of modifications to the fuel storage and magazines to meet Royal Navy requirements before she could commence operations. On completion of modifications and after a short 'work-up', *Dasher* joined FORCE LX, a purely naval force consisting of the aircraft carrier Argus, the cruisers Jamaica and Delhi and four other escorts. The ships departed the Clyde on October 27th 1942. On board *Dasher* were two squadrons, 804 and 891. Both were equipped with six Hurricanes.

FORCE LX joined up with HMS *Furious* and HMS *Biter* who were accompanying a huge convoy comprising forty two liners, merchant ships and escorts. After plunging their way into the Atlantic, the sealed orders were opened to reveal Operation Torch—the invasion of North Africa: destination Oran, Algeria; date and time of arrival, 8th November, 05.30 hours.

En route the large convoy was spotted by an enemy reconnaissance plane. The convoy commander ordered no action against the enemy plane. This puzzled the gunners. However when the plane departed the convoy doubled back on its voyage. It was tactics such as these that ensured that the different convoys, comprising three hundred and twenty seven ships involved in Operation Torch, not one vessel was lost to the dreaded U-boat whilst sailing to North Africa.

On November 8th, after a massive naval bombardment, *Dasher* launched six Sea Hurricanes of 804 Squadron before dawn. Their mission was to escort and defend an Albacore strike on Oran's La Senia airfield.

Although the other part of the escort, 800 Squadron from HMS *Biter* engaged Vichy French fighters, 804 Squadron from *Dasher* did not become involved in action.

Unable to find their return because of the haze, four of the planes from *Dasher* made a forced landing ashore and the other two planes were 'lost' with their pilots. The following day the remnants of *Dasher*'s air group, 891 Squadron, consisting of six Sea Hurricanes, assisted by a few aircraft from Biter, flew fighter patrols over the Oran area. She then left the operational area at dusk with Biter and the aircraft carrier Furious.

The North African invasion was arguably one of the few lights in *Dasher*'s short and ultimately dark career. The following day, 10th November at 12.30 hours saw the surrender of the French and the halt to hostilities throughout Algeria and Morocco. The masters of all assault ships in the invasion force, including *Dasher*, received a message of congratulation from Admiral Cunningham.

After a short stopover in Gibraltar for engine repairs, *Dasher* returned to the Clyde estuary. On arrival at Greenock all aircraft were disembarked before she sailed for Liverpool. Here she was to have repairs to her main engine and to have the air direction room enlarged. Further modifications, prompted by the loss of her sister ship HMS *Avenger*, were made to her bomb room.

While in Liverpool, over the festive season a Christmas party was held on board for the crew's children.

On completion of the work, *Dasher* sailed again for the Clyde to 'work up' for Arctic convoy duties and in February 1943, she arrived in Scapa Flow for operations with the home fleet. Her squadrons at this time comprised 816 and 837 (six Hurricanes plus four Swordfish) with the addition of 891 Squadron (six Hurricanes).

On 15th February 1943 *Dasher* sailed for Murmansk with convoy JW53. The convoy was made up of one hundred and thirty ships and those aboard each vessel were all too aware of the danger attending this voyage, as the enemy had sunk half a million tons of shipping in the Atlantic since the commencement of hostilities.

Two days into the voyage, on February 17th the convoy encountered a violent storm in the North Atlantic. So severe was the storm that it registered Force Eleven—the winds were over seventy miles an hour and the wave height was sixteen metres (fifty four feet). Of the twenty eight freighters in the convoy, six had to turn back. The cruiser Sheffield had a gun turret roof smashed away by the heavy seas breaking over her.

Aboard *Dasher* two of the crew had been lost overboard. The four Hurricanes in the roof of the hangar had worked loose from their tie wires and were smashing into each other. On the hangar deck an eighteen inch torpedo had gone adrift from its couplings and was washing to and fro, in time with the rise and fall of the ship.

The hangar in fact was a complete shambles. Due to the violent rolling and pitching of the ship all security lashings had worked loose. Every aircraft was smashed beyond repair. Spare parts which had been lashed to the ceiling also worked loose and smashed onto the floor of the hangar. With the washing of heavy equipment, parts and armaments, the hangar was placed out of bounds to all members of the crew.

For forty eight hours the aircraft slithered up and down the length

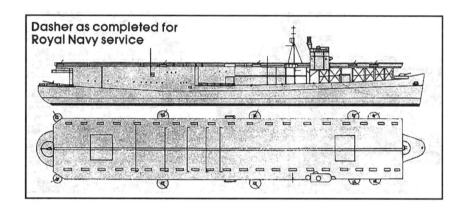

Dasher *off Boston USA (1942)*

of the hangar, sliding from side to side, smashing into each other. On the flight deck two Swordfish planes were tied down and an attempt was made to reinforce the lashings. However this proved to be futile and both aircraft vanished into the stormy Atlantic Ocean.

Sub Lieutenant Brian Bennet watched as the anemometer went off the dial. Then just after midnight the mighty cruel sea forced a split in the ship's side as the American welding came apart. The crew below deck were horrified as they could see the accompanying convoy ships through the split in the side of *Dasher*. The Construction Captain, a member of the Royal Navy Corps of Constructors, notified the Convoy Commander.

The ship was ordered to leave the convoy and take a north west course, passing the east of Iceland.

On entering the safety of Eyjafjord, Iceland, *Dasher* cruised slowly past the small island of Hrisey in the middle of the fjord, before docking at Akureyri, where the welcome shelter allowed temporary repairs to be carried out.

The crew had been genuinely alarmed by the deficiencies of their ship and letters and comments from crewmen seem to express an anxiety beyond the normal so that *Dasher's* reputation as a bad ship was growing. Sailors will quickly draw conclusions from the feel of a vessel and although in wartime conditions, men would be inclined not to worry their loved ones over much, the level of concern is palpable from the following selection of remarks.

"*Dasher* was always in trouble."

"As usual, the engines were a problem."

"Fourteen planes flew off *Dasher* at Operation Torch and not one returned."

"Towards the end of Operation Torch the engine packed up completely for a short spell."

"She had a reputation as a 'problem ship'.

"There was always an air of despondency aboard *Dasher*."

"The ship was always in trouble and not really sea worthy."

"*Dasher* had a reputation of being a 'rogue ship'."

"Nothing ever seemed to be right on the ship."

*slight 'prang' for 891 Squadron aboard* Dasher

*preparing for take-off*

Dasher *in the distance. Convoy in gales off Iceland*
*(photo taken from HMS Blankney)*

*Hurricanes lashed down on* Dasher's *snow covered flight deck in Eyjafjiord,*
*Iceland (February 1943)*

"*Dasher* was a disaster waiting to happen."

"To assist aircraft to land safely in poor visibility, a 'homing device' was installed. This was to prove unsuccessful, as the first plane to use it in misty conditions, never returned. The 'homing device' was dismantled."

"*Dasher* never really 'shook down'."

After she was patched up in Iceland, in what would be her penultimate voyage, *Dasher* sailed to the Caledon yard on the River Tay at Dundee, where permanent repairs to her welding were carried out during the first three weeks of March 1943.

Whilst in Dundee, ominously a fire occurred in the aircraft lift shaft, between the hangar and the flight deck. The cause of the fire was held to be overloading of the lift, all resistors in the electrics becoming hot and igniting old oil lying in the lift shaft.

*Dasher* left Dundee on what was to be her last voyage at the beginning of the fourth week in March 1943. She made for the Clyde and on Saturday 27th March while in a position 205 degrees Cumbrae Island Light 5 miles, approximately half way between Ardrossan and Brodick on the Island of Arran, she blew up and sank within eight minutes, with the loss of three hundred and seventy nine men, 72% of her crew.

CHAPTER 8

# REPERCUSSIONS

When the eyes of the modern reader see the words, aircraft carrier, an association is made. Aircraft carriers mean to us an advanced level of military, naval and aviation science. We see television pictures from recent conflicts in the Gulf and the Adriatic and such places where jet fighters and bombers, timed apparently to perfection, take off and land as if at will. Pilots appear to be skilled scientists and technicians as they interpret bewildering panels of dials. Every possibility seems to be covered by technology as another finely tuned jet speeds off on a mission with its 'smart' weaponry. The organisation of the aircraft carrier itself impresses—teams of highly trained specialists seem to work in harmony to a common purpose. Their tools are the latest that technology has to offer. A mere shift in the breeze would be picked up and responded to by an array of radar and computer controlled equipment.

But life on the Archer class group of escort carriers during the years of World War II was not like this. It will already be evident to the reader that fifty years ago things were a little different, and certainly a good deal less advanced technologically.

Nevertheless the naval authorities were not at all pleased with

117

the outcome of *Dasher*'s career, nor at the consequent loss of life. And in 1943 the Admiralty were not only considering the loss of HMS *Dasher*. They also had the fate of her sister ship HMS *Avenger* on their minds. Avenger was also an American converted escort carrier. On November 15th 1942, she had been hit by a torpedo, fired from the German U-boat *U155*. The torpedo caused a fire on board Avenger, as a result of which a massive explosion took place. The ship was lost along with the lives of 95% of the officers and ratings.

So by March 1943, this Archer class of escort carriers had, between the two vessels lost, accounted for the deaths of over eight hundred fighting men.

When the lease-lend agreement, which provided these ships, was signed between Britain and America, Winston Churchill was reported as having estimated that the Americans could carry out the conversions from merchant ship to aircraft carrier in six months. President Franklin D Roosevelt however stated that they could complete the work in three months. To prove Roosevelt was correct the American shipyards were allowed to work round the clock, seven days a week. It appeared that any shortcuts taken in the design and hasty construction were being paid for heavily in British seamen's lives.

It was recognised by the Deputy Controller at the Admiralty in a secret report issued on April 11th, 1943 that "Safeguards against accidents, such as on *Dasher* are practically non-existent. The safety of these American built carriers was low and the personnel do not seem to have been particularly well trained, nor special precautions taken."

In a written report dated April 30th, 1943 the Deputy Controller accepts the findings of the Board of Enquiry. The report goes on,

> There seems little doubt that the explosion was a petrol vapour one, the sustained 'pouff' being consistent with such explosions. There was no evidence of a 'detonation' type of explosion such as might be occasioned by depth charges or similar types of explosive.
>
> From the damage sustained to the ship it is evident that the

**AMERICAN EMBASSY**
OFFICE OF THE NAVAL ATTACHÉ
LONDON

WRM:HGA

April 22, 1943.

U.S. CONFIDENTIAL
BRITISH SECRET

U.S. CONFIDENTIAL - BRITISH SECRET

My dear Sir Henry:

  It would be greatly appreciated if this office could be furnished with a copy of the report of the Board of Enquiry on H.M.S. DaSHER, when same becomes available.

  It would further be appreciated if this office could be informed of any alterations, particularly to the petrol systems, which the Admiralty may authorize on this type of vessel.

    Yours sincerely,

    T. A. SOLBERG,
    Captain, U.S. Navy.

Sir Henry V. Markham, K.C.B.,
Permanent Secretary,
Board of Admiralty,
Admiralty,
London, S.W.1.

*terse note*

119

SECRET

5th May, 1943.

Dear Captain Solberg,

In reply to your letter of the 22nd April, No: 5111, the report of the board of inquiry into the loss of H.M.S.DASHER has only recently been received and is now under consideration at the Admiralty. When our examination is completed I shall be pleased to let you have a copy of the report and to inform you of any alterations which it may be decided to make in this type of vessel.

Believe me,
Yours very truly,

Captain T.A.Solberg, U.S.N.,
Office of the Naval Attache,
American Embassy,
1, Grosvenor Square,
W.1.

*Sir Henry Markham's delayed reply to the Americans*

cause of the explosion was a large one consistent to a partial filling at least of the petrol compartment with vapour.

The causes of the presence and ignition of the vapour are not apparent but due to the inadequate safety arrangements in this class of ship may have been many.

The loss of *Dasher* badly affected Anglo-American relations when the Admiralty ordered modifications to the American designed aviation gasoline systems of *Dasher*'s sister ships. In the same report of April 30th, the Deputy Controller at the Admiralty made clear that the fault lay not on the British side of the Atlantic.

As pointed out in my memo DNE 6321/43 of 11th April, safeguards against accidents of this nature are, by our standards, practically non-existent in the petrol arrangements and the hangars of these American built escort ships. Steps have been taken to rectify this state of affairs in all classes so far as is practicable, but this will take time and will mainly devolve on our resources. B.A.D. Washington has been kept fully informed and asked to do what he can to get things rectified in new ships before delivery.

The Admiralty blamed the Americans for the disaster. The Americans in turn blamed the British. In a memo at the time the US authorities stated that the disaster was caused by,

The lack of British experience with bulk aviation fuel.

The level of official recrimination was high. Among ordinary seamen these escort carriers were already the subject of unease and ridicule. The already lost *Avenger* and *Dasher*—as well as the still operational and vital, *Archer, Activity, Biter, Battler, Hunter, Attacker* and *Stalker*— were known among the ratings in those days as 'Woolworth's Carriers'. At that time, Woolworth's stores sold very few items over the cost of six old pennies. Everything purchased from Woolworth's was cheap. Likewise it was the general opinion of those who built

121

and those who served on these ships that everything was done 'on the cheap'.

Having received the Board of Enquiry report, the Commander in Chief of the Home Fleet sent out a secret memo to all other ships in *Dasher's* class. Its contents, which were for immediate implementation, are worth quoting in full. They point to the cause of what went wrong and the great loss of life. The contents may have given some reassurance to the officers and ratings working on the sister ships under what must have been feelings of unease.

1   As a result of the investigations into the loss of HMS *Dasher* it has been proved that the cause of the disaster was due to internal explosion, probably petrol.

2   Certain alterations to petrol stowage arrangements have been recommended.

3   The following immediate precautions are to be taken:–

   (a)   The trunk giving access to the forward end of the shaft tunnel is not to be used.

   (b)   The watertight door giving access from the Engine Room to the shaft tunnel is to be kept permanently closed.

   (c)   Rigid observance of the magazine and petrol regulations is to be enforced.

   (d)   All defects in petrol systems are to be reported to the Commanding Officer immediately they are disclosed.

   (e)   Commanding Officers are to ensure that the Engineer Officer in charge of the petrol system enforces rigid discipline in his organisation.

   (f)   Smoking on the messdeck over the petrol hold is to be forbidden.

   (g)   Particular attention is to be paid to keeping the bilges in the petrol compartment pumped dry so that the exhaust ventilating trunks are free from obstruction.

   (h)   Life belts are invariably to be worn when ships are under way.

(i)    Calcium flares are not to be used in life floats, life buoys or life belts. Any calcium flares which it is desired to retain on board are to be kept in a watertight container.

This last precaution was included it is thought, because the calcium flares may have been responsible for igniting the aviation fuel in the water. Those men who perhaps thought they had made good their escape from the sinking ship were then caught up in an inferno on the surface of the water.

As a result of the experience with *Dasher* the British navy agreed to modify the petrol arrangements in these ships 'in accordance with normal British practice'. Acknowledging the amount of work involved and the time required to carry it out under a heavy programme of operational duties, a number of alterations were ordered as an interim measure.

Again quoting from the document signed by the Deputy Naval Commander and stamped 14 May 1943 is instructive of where it was believed that the problem lay.

... the following alterations are being undertaken as an interim measure.
(1) (a)  Reduce the amount of petrol carried to about 36,000 galls. The tanks not required for petrol to be filled with water and pipes blanked off.
    (b)  Fit artificial exhaust ventilation to the hangar (inductor system).
    (c)  Fit inductor ventilation to the petrol control compartment and cleavage gauge compartment.
    (d)  Fit inductor ventilation to the petrol hold. (In Archer and Biter only).
    (e)  Raise the general ship ventilation fans which are fitted in the hangar to positions as high as practicable above the 8' line. Fit spray shields to these fans.
    (f)  Make doors leading to funnel uptake compartment, blower compartment etc gastight.

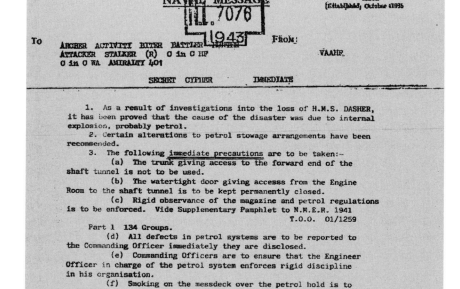

NAVAL MESSAGE
1943
7076

1220L
[Established] October 1936

To
ARCHER ACTIVITY BITER BATTLER
ATTACKER STALKER (R) O in C HF
O in C WA ADMIRALTY 401

From:
VAAHF

SECRET CYPHER          IMMEDIATE

1. As a result of investigations into the loss of H.M.S. DASHER, it has been proved that the cause of the disaster was due to internal explosion, probably petrol.

2. Certain alterations to petrol stowage arrangements have been recommended.

3. The following immediate precautions are to be taken:-

(a) The trunk giving access to the forward end of the shaft tunnel is not to be used.

(b) The watertight door giving accesss from the Engine Room to the shaft tunnel is to be kept permanently closed.

(c) Rigid observance of the magazine and petrol regulations is to be enforced. Vide Supplementary Pamphlet to N.M.E.R. 1941
T.O.O.  01/1259
Part 1  134 Groups.

(d) All defects in petrol systems are to be reported to the Commanding Officer immediately they are disclosed.

(e) Commanding Officers are to ensure that the Engineer Officer in charge of the petrol system enforces rigid discipline in his organisation.

(f) Smoking on the messdeck over the petrol hold is to be forbidden.

(g) Particular attention is to be paid to keeping the bilges in the petrol compartment pumped dry so that the exhaust ventilating trunks are free from obstruction.

(h) Life belts are invariably to be worn when ships are under way.

(j) Calcium flares are not to be used in life floats, life buoys or life belts. Any calcium flares which it is desired to retain on board are to be kept in a watertight container.

*secret message*

    (g)    Fit protective casing to exposed petrol piping on ships' side outboard.

    (h)    Remove existing wiring from the cleavage gauge compartment and use magazine hand lamps pattern 8815.

    (i)    Remove existing wiring from the petrol control compartment and fit exterior light box in accordance with British practice.

  (2)    Fit asbestos fire curtains in the hangar as usual in British practice.

  (3)    Blank door leading from engine room to shaft tunnel.

In a letter dated 19th May 1943, along with the Board of Enquiry report, the above information was sent by Sir Henry V Markham, Permanent Secretary at the Board of Admiralty to Captain T A Solberg in the office of the Naval Attaché at the American Embassy in London's Grosvenor Square. With those changes to be made 'in accordance with British practice' one can only wonder, with all the implied criticism of the Americans, just how it was received.

It may have been some small consolation to the bereaved and to all those caught up in the enquiry and the aftermath that the part played by *Dasher*'s sister escort carriers was considerable.

The work of *Biter, Archer, Pursuer, Activity, Battler, Stalker* and *Hunter* and others in the North Atlantic greatly reduced the sinkings of Allied ships. In May 1943 Germany lost thirty eight U-boats in one of which the German Admiral Doenitz lost his son Peter. On 24th May 1943 Admiral Doenitz ordered his U-boats out of the North Atlantic to recover. In his memoirs, he was to write of that day, "We had lost the battle of the Atlantic."

CHAPTER 9

# ASSESSING THE EVIDENCE

The minutes of the proceedings and the findings of the Board of
Enquiry into the loss of *Dasher*, at this distance of time, may appear
to give a plausible explanation of the catastrophe. Although far from
satisfactory in any sense, at least a reason for death and destruction
helps to explain. For most people whose lives were touched by these
terrible events however, there was no such comfort.

All of the proceedings of the Board of Enquiry were conducted in
secret. Even survivors had no means of knowing what had happened.
Talking to survivors in the writing of this book, it was evident that
some had not even any clear idea who of their shipmates had survived
and who had perished. Other seamen on the sister ships had no
formal information to go on. All naval personnel were ordered not
even to talk about the disaster.

The local population likewise had nothing substantial to help them
interpret the events. Those who had witnessed the explosion or who
had seen the casualties being brought ashore and even seen the
funeral procession could only piece together such scraps of
information that were to hand.

Some of the rumours and stories which circulated about the

disaster and about the cause should be addressed. Among the stories which are still alive to some degree are that *Dasher* was sunk by an enemy mine; she was the victim of 'friendly fire' from a torpedo fired from one of the many British ships then on the Clyde. The U-boat torpedo theory is still given credence in the minds of some. Some said that *Dasher* could have been sabotaged by a bomb placed on board when in Belfast. And the 'blame the victim' explanation is still voiced—that the explosion was caused by a member of the crew smoking in a restricted area.

An enemy mine was highly unlikely. The shipping channels in the Clyde were regularly swept for mines. Other ships had sailed these waters that day, before and after the explosion without mishap. In any case Ardrossan was the busiest minesweeping base in Scotland.

The friendly fire cause is also unlikely—no record can be found of any other ship working with torpedoes in the vicinity.

As the extract of the letter from the German U-boat archive in Cuxhaven shows, no U-boats were on the Clyde that day and there is no record that any U-boats were involved. As for the IRA theory, *Dasher* had never ever been in Belfast to have had a bomb planted. And the member of crew smoking explanation is also most improbable. Even the most neglectful of sailors would have been extremely foolish to ignore the No Smoking signs on what was known as a 'floating fuel station'.

Among the more probable causes put forward over the years since 1943 have been an engine room fire leading to the explosion. Possible sources of such a fire in the engine room have been identified as the engine crank case blowing up; an electrical fault; or metal to metal contact creating a spark and igniting fuel vapour. The other major theory as to the cause of the explosion has been the view that an aircraft crashed while attempting to land on the carrier.

**Engine crank case blowing up**

Six of the ship's crew made the following observation at the Board of Enquiry:

**Stiftung Traditionsarchiv Unterseeboote**

# U=Boot=Archiv

Cuxhaven-Altenbruch, 227.09.1994

Mr. John Steele
104 Eglinton Road
Ardrossan
KA22 8NN
Scotland

Dear Mr. Steele,-

Thank you for your letter of 21st Sept.1994
and the enclosure of envelope for answer,- but no return-postage (see reverse side)

(I) To answer your request I enclose. :

1. The british escort-carrier DASHER is destroyed at 27th March 1943 on the
2. River Clyde  as a result of a petrol explosion and fire.
3. Ther was no German U-Boot near to that,- and no German U-Boot was involved.
4.
5.
6.

*The U-boat archive discounts one suggested cause.*

*The archive also confirmed that the German authorities knew of* Dasher's *fate 'very soon' after the ship sank*

Lt Commander Lane's first thoughts were, "there had been an explosion in the engine room boiler up-takes, as it was similar to previous explosions of that nature."

Lt Commander Wootton was in the engine room at the time of the explosion and he stated, "It was a long explosion, similar to when the port engine crank case blew out."

Able Seaman Harold Martin said, "It seemed like a boiler blowing up."

Able Seaman Tom Hunter stated, "It seemed like a blow back from the engine."

Able Seaman George Reynolds was in the engine room and saw "a flash coming along between the port and starboard engines."

Ordinary Seaman Michael Drury said, "I thought the explosion was from the engine room."

## Electrical fault

The Board of Enquiry ascertained that the lighting system was, "not up to magazine lighting specification and that a fault in the system could have ignited petrol vapours when lights were switched on or off."

## Metal to metal spark

The Admiralty were of the opinion that the safety of the American built carriers was low and that the personnel were not particularly trained, nor special precautions taken. Due to this lack of safety training, did someone strike metal to metal causing a spark which could have ignited the petrol vapours?

Lt Commander Wootton saw the fire and flames shoot out from the bottom of the engine room after bulkheads. Many engine room personnel and other crew members witnessed the fire in the engine room. It would appear to be safe to assume that the engine room was on fire.

We also know that

1 the aircraft carrier had 75,000 gallons of fuel on board;
2 the aviation fuel tanks were full;
3 twenty four depth charges were in the hangar, twelve feet from the aircraft lift;
4 twelve depth charges were stored adjacent to the platform;
5 three torpedoes were stored on either side of the lift well, starboard;
6 three torpedoes were in the rack, portside;
7 all warheads were facing the stern of the ship (where the engine room is situated);
8 sixty eight depth charges were stored in a hatch, forward of the lift well;
9 the aircraft were being refuelled (immediately above the engine room);
10 the ship was fully laden with ammunition for the aircraft guns, the ship's 4" AA guns, four 40mm guns and eight 20mm guns;
11 we know that there was a drip from the fuel tank. The drip was noticed two weeks before the explosion. It was never reported that it had been rectified. The rate of drip was once every five seconds (ie thirty per minute, 1800 per hour);
12 six of the fuel tanks were situated in the engine room; the remainder were directly below; all tanks were full.

Lt Commander G W Dobson of *La Capricieuse*, Sub Lt E C D Holeman on *Dasher*'s motor launch *ML 528* and Leading Supply Assistant Harold W Baker all stated that they heard two explosions. If a second explosion took place, any one of the above, numbered one to twelve, could have been the cause.

## An aircraft crash during landing

There are eye witnesses from Ardrossan, West Kilbride, Seamill and the Isle of Arran who all support the cause as being an aircraft crash. Alex Buchanan of Motherwell was a radar instructor aboard the training ship *Isle of Sark* which was involved in the rescue operation.

Alex wrote to a national newspaper that "the popular theory on our ship was that one of *Dasher*'s aircraft had crashed on landing and had caused a torpedo to explode."

P A Marsden of Southampton had joined *Dasher* at Liverpool in January 1943. He wrote to a local newspaper relating his experiences aboard the aircraft carrier. "A Swordfish missed the flight deck when landing. It hit the quarter deck and caused the depth charges which were stored there to explode."

The computer print out for HMS *Dasher* from the Wrecks Section, Ministry of Defence states, "Sank following petrol fire and explosion thought to have been caused by an aircraft attempting to land on carrier."

Monsignor Barry of North Berwick is compiling a manuscript entitled *Naval Battles that Never Were*. His research states,

> Two hundred and fifty naval personnel who had been transported to the United States to join ships of the Attacker class at Pascagoula Naval Yard on the Gulf of Mexico, heard a strong rumour about the sinking of *Dasher*. They heard that one of *Dasher*'s aircraft was preparing to land on the carrier at 1648 hours. The rumour was that the pilot misjudged his height on approach to the carrier and instead of landing on the deck, the plane plunged into the space between quarter deck and the flight deck.

This would certainly have explained the "muffled rumbling report" and the suddenness of the explosion. It would also have explained the smoke seen belching out between the flight deck and the quarter deck. Monsignor Barry goes on,

> That such an accident could happen was proved on 1st April 1944 when an Avenger aircraft, having developed a defect in its depth charge sacks, was attempting to land on HMS *Tracker*. It missed the flight deck and flew straight into the round down. The aircraft burst into flames, setting off ammunition in the aircraft and round the ship's Bofors gun.

Finally the aircraft engine fell onto the quarter deck, starting a dangerous fire. Safety precautions, newly installed, and efficient damage limitation prevented a repetition of the *Dasher* disaster.

Whatever the initial cause of fire on board *Dasher*—be it an engine problem, an electrical fault, a metal on metal spark or indeed an aircraft crash landing—there seems little doubt that the Board of Enquiry was correct in concluding that the initial explosion was in the area of the petrol flat. The 'rumbling' explosion would probably be different from a detonation of high explosive.

Circumstances have changed in the half century since the *Dasher* disaster, not least in public attitudes to liability. Whereas in 1943 under wartime conditions the survivors and bereaved relatives may have felt a lingering sense of injustice, or at least confusion, a similar loss of life today, it is safe to say, would result in 528 legal actions against the authorities.

In compiling all the evidence and material for this book, some modern day legal opinion might be instructive. All of the relevant papers were looked at by a practising solicitor who has knowledge of maritime affairs. Bill Haggerty of Ayr served as a deck officer aboard the Cunard Brockelbank Line.

He gained the impression that there was on *Dasher* insufficient awareness of the dangers that could be caused by a build-up of gas from the stored aviation fuel. "Gas from aviation fuel," he explained, "escapes, even from 'liquid tight' containers. There is no doubt that a container with a drip from a joint of the type described in the evidence by Lt Commander Wootton— a drip every five seconds— would produce a dangerous measure of inflammable gas."

It sounded to Bill Haggerty that the authorities may have been rather casual in their apprach to the elimination of this drip. According to the minutes of the Board of Enquiry, a Sub Lieutenant was told it was leaking and to get something done about it, but Lt Commander Wootton was unable to say if anything had been done

The findings seem to suggest that only a lighted cigarette or perhaps an electrical fault.could have caused the explosion. But even a spark from metal on metal could have set it off. Certainly by early 1945 when my ship regularly carried a full cargo of 100 octane in 44 gallon drums and jerry cans the holds were degassed several times a day. All shoes worn had to have rubber soles and heels and the cargo hooks and the lower ends of the wires were covered in canvas to prevent sparks when loading and unloading.

One result of the *Dasher* disaster seems to have been a greater awareness of the potential danger of petroleum vapour build-up in enclosed spaces on escort carriers. One must however, bear in mind that such precautions were already enforced on purpose built fleet carriers and that *Dasher* and her like were hastily converted in the United States from tankers or other cargo hulls.

But just as important in assessing the evidence of the disaster and looking at the improvements in safety procedures is the human dimension. In the Britain of 1943 the psychological impact on all kinds of individuals caught up in the disaster and its aftermath was not generally considered. For a start the nation was at war and individual needs were felt to be subordinate to the cause of the greater national good.

It is true also that what is now known as post traumatic stress disorder was unheard of then. This condition is now well researched and documented and develops after an individual has experienced a traumatic event, either as a victim, a witness or as a member of the rescue services exposed to the horror of the aftermath. The symptoms are similar to neurotic conditions and can include visual difficulties, paralysis of limbs, tremors, facial tics and involuntary movements. A distancing from family, close relatives and sleep disturbance can occur.

A common feature of the condition is a re-experiencing of the event during nightmares and in daytime flashbacks. It is common too for an insignificant noise to cause an exaggerated response and a stressful reliving of the incident. These symptoms may occur for decades after the event and are now minimised where possible by counselling and sensitive handling after the event.

According to psychological opinion, even allowing for wartime restrictions, the authorities did not manage things well after the *Dasher* tragedy. While many of the statements by survivors, relatives and others who were touched by these events show a strength and courage at the distance of fifty years, the pain too is there for all to see.

Organising an inquiry aboard an identical ship within three days could have been an enormously insensitive act. Survivors called to give evidence, having been plucked from a burning sea, witnessing shipmates die around them displays to the modern mind, an unbelievable lack of understanding and sensitivity. The crew who were interviewed had neither legal nor moral support and in certain cases were recalled for further interrogation with the implication of blame. This may well have had long term ramifications for the victims.

In a sense however, bad though this reliving of events was on an identical sister ship, the witnesses to the board of inquiry may have been the most privileged in the task of overcoming the experience. However limited, at least they had the chance to talk about what had happened and to hear others talk about it. For most other people involved this was not possible, as in the quest for secrecy it was actively discouraged. It has been clear in the writing of this book that some of the survivors and the bereaved relatives have been carrying these scars to the present day.

# Sub Lt Lionel Godfrey RNVR

891 Squadron HMS *Dasher*

From mid-December '42 until the end of January 1943 No 891 Squadron was based mainly at the Royal Naval Air Station at Machrihanish on the Mull of Kintyre. There we continued to keep the squadron at full operational strength until rejoining *Dasher* for the now familiar role of protecting a convoy bound for Russia. The severity of the weather at this time kept our flying to a minimum, but the mere presence of an escort carrier with the convoy proved a deterrent to enemy attacks by air or by submarine.

Apart from the really wicked weather and roaring Arctic seas which caused *Dasher* to spring a leak well below the water-line, this particular convoy protection operation was relatively uneventful. On our return to Scapa Flow our ship was ordered to proceed to the Clyde for repair while we were shore-based once more at Machrihanish awaiting orders to rejoin *Dasher* following the completion of her minor repairs.

We enjoyed our short time at Machrihanish . It was always a good, hospitable place where the station officers and men welcomed our presence among them and did their best to help us relax from operational duty. Had we known what was about to happen to some of us within minutes of leaving Machrihanish none of us would have wanted to stay anywhere else but on the Mull of Kintyre.

The day before *Dasher* took up her operational duties once more, four of our Hurricanes, their pilots and almost all of the maintenance personnel had been taken aboard by lighter as the ship swung at anchor in the Firth of Clyde. The following day Max Newman, myself and two other pilots were circling the carrier as she worked up speed into wind preparatory to us landing, when *Dasher* exploded before our very eyes and sank from view within four minutes. In my mind's eye I can still see the lift being hurled some two to three hundred feet in the air and bodies falling from its surface into the sea. There was absolutely nothing that we could do except keep radio silence and return to Machrihanish where our Commanding Officer reported verbally what we had witnessed.

891 Squadron, left with only four aircraft, four pilots and less than a dozen maintenance personnel, was disbanded almost immediately from Machrihanish . Two days later I ended up taking compulsory leave in London with no appointment or designation to another squadron or to a shore base. It was a sad end to what had been a happy association with an efficient fighter squadron. At no time since the tragic end of HMS *Dasher* have I heard of or seen an official acknowledgement of her loss.

After four weeks leave without pay and without notice of an appointment back to duty I visited a branch of the Admiralty in Queen Anne's Mansions, London in an endeavour to learn what I should do with myself. From a Commander seated behind a desk in a depressing looking office I received a flat denial that anything untoward had happened to *Dasher* or to 891 Squadron. When I, a mere Sub Lieutenant (A) RNVR, protested that with my own eyes I'd seen *Dasher* go down and disappear beneath the calm waters of the Firth of Clyde, the only response I got from the severe looking Commander was "Nonsense! You'd better get yourself a casual payment and remain on indefinite leave. You'll be informed when you're needed."

## Bill Spence, Lochranza, Arran

## Bill Dickie J P, Brodick, Arran

We had been to a bring and buy sale in the public hall, Brodick. The sale had commenced at 2pm on that sunny Saturday afternoon. On leaving the hall, we went down to the seafront to watch the ships as, like most other teenage boys, we were shipping enthusiasts.

We spent some time watching the various types of vessels going about their business. There were two Coasters in the area as well as an aircraft carrier. Circling the aircraft carrier was a motor launch which must have been on duty as aircraft were flying off, then landing back on the carrier.

This activity was of special interest to us, especially the planes. We watched one plane "flying off", then it circled and approached the ship. It came very low, in fact it was below the level of the flight-deck. It flew towards the carrier and then disappeared, we assumed that it was flying past the other side of the ship at low level.

We watched the bow of the ship for the re-appearance of the plane, however it never came in view. Just then, we heard a deep rumble, followed by an explosion. Within seconds, smoke was billowing from the stern.

The ship started to go down by the stern then it very slowly disappeared. A few seconds later, the sea went on fire. We just could not believe what we were witnessing. At Brodick Pier, the Royal Navy vessel, which was locally known as "The Contraband Ship" put to sea, to assist in the rescue operation. The two coasters diverted from their courses and made for the disaster area.

The rescue ships went as close as they could to the high flames and dense black smoke. We could not see anyone in the water, due to the distance, however by the activity of the various rescue vessels, we knew that a major rescue operation was in progress.

After some time had elapsed, darkness started to fall and we made our way home for our supper. Later that evening, we heard the sound of the "Contraband Ship" returning. We cycled down to Brodick Pier to await its arrival. When it berthed, we could see markings on the deck, markings where bodies had lain. The crew were visibly upset and they told us that they had removed many bodies from the water and transferred them to another Royal Navy ship which had taken them to Ardrossan.

Both of us firmly believe it was the low flying plane that had crashed into the ship, beneath the flight-deck, which had been the cause of the sea disaster.

We were both born on Arran and we have lived all our lives on the island. *(Bill Spence was a grocer for 42 years and also served on Caledonian MacBrayne ferries for 8 years. Bill Dickie worked as a postman on the island for 44 years and is a Justice of the Peace.)*

## Mrs Mary Ingles

Mauchline, Ayrshire

I am the widow of Alexander Ingles. He was a sergeant in the Scots Guards, second battalion 1944–48. His father was a policeman in West Kilbride for twenty eight years, from 1924–1952.

My father was also a policeman. Alex was an accountant and when he was a young boy, he was very keen on ship spotting. He and his brother would go up to the field at the rear of the police bungalow in Seamill, to watch the ships.

Alex told me many times how he and his brother witnessed the sinking of an aircraft carrier. I can still hear my husband's voice saying,

"The planes had been taking off and landing all day. Then this one, on landing, went right down the hold of the aircraft carrier. There was an explosion then a pall of black smoke. In a very few minutes, the ship was gone."

My husband was so adamant about what he saw and he had a penchant for detail, due to his profession as an accountant. Sadly, he never ever knew the name of the ship before he died in February 1991.

CHAPTER 10

# UNSUNG HEROES

| | |
|---|---|
| Petty Officer Stamp. | HMS *Dasher* |
| Petty Officer Terry | HMS *Dasher* |
| Lt Commander Lane | HMS *Dasher* |
| Daniel Gaffney | HMS *Dasher* |
| Petty Officer Jeff Gray | HMS *Dasher* |
| Lt Commander Dobson | *FS La Capricieuse* |
| | 19 survivors |
| Captain Terretta | SS *Lithium* |
| | 60 survivors |
| Captain McNair | HMS *Isle of Sark* |
| | recovered 35, 3 of whom died, 32 survivors |
| Sub Lt E C D Holeman RNVR | *Motor Launch 528,* 40 survivors |
| Sub Lt. R F C Durbin RNVR | |
| The Captain | SS *Cragsman* |

The Unknown Heroes
    Countless acts of heroism were never revealed and it is only but fair and just that they are recorded.

**Petty Officer C J Terry**      **Telegraphist**
**Petty Officer Stamp**      **RNVR**

Both officers were below deck, amidst buckled doors, burst plates sprung from the ship's sides and in complete darkness, with the exception of flickering light from the many fires.

The Abandon Ship! order had been announced by Captain Boswell. However both officers remained below deck assisting young ratings to safety. These officers displayed outstanding courage and heroism, putting their lives at risk, aboard a sinking ship, to ensure that their shipmates were given the best possible chance to survive.

The ship was sinking extremely fast but both remained where they were, helping others to escape. In doing so they lost their lives.

### Lt Commander Lane

Lt Commander Lane was ordered to "Find out what is happening!" He made his way down to the engine room. The further down he went, the more damage, heat and danger he encountered. One deck was found to be three feet under water with the sea pouring in.

Realising that he could go no further, he retraced his steps along the darkened passageways, back to the deck. As he made his way to safety he stopped and checked every office and cabin on his route, to ensure that they were empty.

On jumping overboard he swam about the survivors in the water and in the Carley Floats shouting encouragingly with the words, "It will be alright lads. We will soon be out."

When a rescue boat arrived on the scene, the crew threw ropes to those in the water. However, due to the coldness of the sea and the length of time in the water, the survivors' hands were numb. As a result they were having difficulty grasping and holding onto the ropes. Lt Commander Lane swam about tying a bowline knot onto the ropes, thereby ensuring that the struggling could hold onto the ropes or put them over themselves and be pulled toward the rescue vessels.

Whilst swimming about during the rescue operation, the Lt

Commander discarded all of his clothes as they were not only slowing him down from swimming from Carley float to Carley float, they were also pulling him under.

a) The Lt Commander risked his life when checking the offices and cabins prior to jumping overboard.

b) Whilst in the water he risked his life swimming about the Carley floats shouting words of encouragement.

c) He could have boarded a rescue boat but instead he remained in the water tying knots in the ropes to save others.

## Heroes in the messdeck

The crew members "formed an orderly queue" to go through the watertight door and make their way to safety, whilst the ship was in darkness and sinking by the stern. By acting in this manner with no sign of panic, these men upheld the highest standards in keeping with seafaring traditions.

## Sub Lt E C D Holeman RNVR

In command of *Dasher*'s motor-launch MV *528*

On witnessing the explosion and seeing the aircraft-lift "flying into the air", he went to Crash Stations immediately, made for *Dasher* and picked up a total of forty men; eighteen were in the water and twenty were in Carley rafts.

## Captain & crew SS *Cragsman*—a Coaster built in Paisley (1924)

The flotilla of rescue vessels were stopped at the perimeter of the dense smoke and searing flames when they witnessed the Cragsman disappear into the billowing smoke. Fearing the worst for the coaster, they were most relieved to see the Cragsman reappear laden with survivors.

At the conclusion of the rescue operation, the skipper of the coaster transferred those he had saved on to a Royal Navy vessel. The Cragsman then slipped away quietly, to continue on her voyage.

The unknown skipper never ever reported taking part in the very dangerous rescue operation and his actions were never made known to the public or the survivors.

### Petty Officer Jeffery R Gray

On jumping into the water, he made for the Carley rafts which were furthest away, thereby enabling his shipmates who were not such good swimmers to make for the nearby rafts.

Whilst swimming in the water, he and another crew member assisted a rating who had been injured by swimming over to him and assisting him to the raft. On reaching the raft, they both helped the injured seaman to board the raft, after which PO Gray boarded and cradled the casualty's head on his lap whilst they were waiting to be saved.

There is no doubt that but for PO Gray's action, the seaman would have perished.

### Captain J H McNair RN

In command of HMS *Isle of Sark* (a radar training ship)

The Isle of Sark was four and a half miles from *Dasher* when the ship "blew up". On immediately turning towards her and heading at full speed, they watched as the aircraft carrier disappeared. Shortly afterwards a flame was seen followed by a big fire.

They saw two rafts, with those on board paddling with their feet and hands, to get as far away as possible from the flames.

Captain McNair stopped his ship just short of the "sea of fire" and ordered his lifeboats to be lowered. At that point a small coaster (the Cragsman) sailed right into the smoke and flames to pick up survivors.

The Isle of Sark picked up thirty five survivors of whom three were unconscious. Artificial respiration was applied for some considerable time but the three could not be revived.

Number of survivors brought ashore at Ardrossan—thirty two.

### Daniel Gaffney

A member of HMS *Dasher* crew from Glasgow

Whilst in the water, he pulled an unconscious shipmate toward a raft. Then with the assistance of an airman swam over to another crew member and brought him alongside the raft. He was also injured.

143

### Lt Commander G W Dobson RNR

In command of *La Capricieuse*

His lifeboats plucked twenty six survivors out of the sea. Unfortunately seven of them died by the time they berthed at Ardrossan.

### Captain J F Terretta

In command of SS *Lithium* (Built 1917)

Owned by Imperial Chemical Industries Ltd, Fleetwood

Whilst on passage from Glasgow to Llanddulas, SS *Lithium* was 1/4 of a mile from *Dasher* when the explosion took place. A bright flash appeared and dense smoke issued from the stern.

Captain Terretta turned his ship around to render what assistance they could. The captain and his crew saved sixty men from a watery grave. The men were then placed aboard the HMS *Sir Galahad*.

At 18.30 hours the SS *Lithium* having disembarked the survivors, proceeded on her voyage.

CHAPTER 11

# IN REMEMBRANCE

In 1992 Mr John Hall of Stewarton, Ayrshire wrote to the Royal Naval Association, Scottish Area enquiring why there was no memorial to the three hundred and seventy nine officers and ratings who perished when the Aircraft Carrier HMS *Dasher* was lost in the Clyde Estuary in the spring of 1943.

The Association, under the guidance of the chairman, Mac Mackay, reacted swiftly. The funding was organised for a memorial, a large military parade, a church Remembrance Service and a Dedication Service.

The organisation of the event took seven months. *Dasher's* operational career lasted seven months.

On Saturday 27 March 1993, fifty years to the day of the sea disaster a number of events took place.

Security arrangements were increased for the parade and church service in light of a recent bombing at Warrington. With such a large gathering of past and present servicemen, Strathclyde Police decided not to take any chances.

Prior to the largest parade ever to march in Ardrossan, motorists were instructed not to park in Glasgow Street or Princess Street as these streets would feature on the route. Portable bins were removed and Barony St John's Church was checked for explosive devices.

Fifty years of sadness were finally laid to rest in Ardrossan on Saturday 27 March 1993 with the unveiling of a permanent memorial to those who perished in the war-time tragedy on the Firth of Clyde.

In the first public recognition in half a century, Ardrossan town centre came to a standstill for the duration of a moving public tribute to the sacrifice of 27 officers and 352 others who lost their lives on the sinking aircraft carrier, HMS *Dasher*.

Emotions ran high as the grief that survivors, relatives and townsfolk had stored up for five decades was finally and unashamedly set free.

The sadness that people had felt was suddenly lifted through the unveiling of a lasting memorial to the HMS *Dasher* and her crew, whose lives were cruelly cut short on that fateful March afternoon at the height of the Second World War.

The day was organised by the Royal Naval Association Scottish Area and was attended by survivors and relatives from all over Britain. Perhaps the furthest travelled were Joan and John Hook who flew over from Harare in Zimbabwe to remember Joan's brother who was lost on the *Dasher*.

The sheer scale of the disaster was kept quiet due to wartime reporting restrictions but hundreds of stories were swapped at the first public recognition of the incident.

A parade of ex-servicemen, relatives, Air Training Corps and youth groups marched through the town before a moving service conducted by the Reverend Sandy Young took place in Barony St John's Church.

In attendance were the Royal Navy's Commodore Clyde, Commodore John Trewby, Lord Lieutenant for Ayrshire and Arran, Major Richard Henderson and dignitaries from Cunninghame District Council. The Guard was provided by HMS *Gannet* and the music was performed by HMS *Neptune* Volunteer Band.

"One of the healthy beliefs of the people of scriptural times," said the Reverend Sandy Young in his sermon, "was that the

*Fifty years on—relatives of those who perished & survivors lay wreaths at the inauguration of a memorial stone in Ardrossan on 27th March 1993*

mourning and the honouring of the dead should be public, that the process of remembering, grieving, and coming to terms with loss is enabled by the story being told. We read from Ezekiel (27.29–31), how the mariners gathered by the sea shore to remember the men, to retell the story, and to weep for the lost merchant ships of Tarshish."

"In contrast," the Rev Young went on, "the many losses of wartime had to be borne in the context of an ongoing conflict . . . each survivor and relative must handle grief privately while continuing to bear the burden of war.

"Surely today is overdue to HMS *Dasher* and her ship's company. We have shared the story and celebrated the service of men and vessel."

A moving dedication service and wreath laying ceremony was held after the church service in Ardrossan's sunken garden. The pink granite stone was unveiled by Mrs Mackay, wife of Royal Naval Association Scottish Area chairman Mr T Mackay, Commodore Trewby and *Dasher* survivor James McGloin of Ayr.

And out of the inhospitable grey sky, five helicopters from HMS *Gannet* 891 Squadron burst through the sea mist to perform a breathtaking fly past with headlights blazing.

Earlier, they had dropped wreaths on behalf of the Royal Navy and the RAF over the spot where *Dasher* now lies.

Of the many bouquets of flowers laid at the memorial, one came from an Ardrossan woman who had received it on Mother's Day. She had wanted to lay them for all the mothers of the men on *Dasher* who didn't come back.

And on the following day the Royal Naval Association presented the ship's badge of the present day HMS *Dasher* to the congregation of Barony St John's Church to mark that the service had taken place there. This is now on permanent view for anyone wishing to visit the church.

Afterwards, event organiser Mr Mackay said, "It was a moving day that was absolutely out of this world and I can't thank people enough for all their support. It was something that had to be done and during the day, all the sadness was lifted when at long last there was something for people to come and see. It's incredible that all this was done in only seven months, and after speaking to all the survivors and families who visited for the occasion, I was told that the people of Ardrossan were the friendliest and most helpful people they had met.

"It was as if the people of the town were old friends and I can't thank them enough for their interest and support.

"It really helped to make the day a memorable occasion for everyone involved."

On Saturday 16 July 1994 a further memorial plaque was unveiled by Robert Dotchin, survivor and John Steele, author of this book. The service and unveiling took place at St Peter's Church, Ardrossan.

The young men and women of Ardrossan Sea Cadets 612 were in attendance to pay their respects. After the dedication of the memorial by Father Lynch the address was given by the author, who helped organise the event.

The plaque is mounted on the west-facing wall, opposite the waters where the disaster took place.

An annual reunion of what has come to be known as "the *Dasher* Family" is now held in Ardrossan. The families come together and after a church service they lay wreaths at the memorial stone, then retire to a local hotel for a meal and an exchange of stories and memories of those that were lost.

# Chapter 12

# DASHER SHIPMATES

There are several reasons why the writing of this book was undertaken. Trying to understand events that took place over half a century ago should not be dismissed lightly. It is important for all kinds of reasons to know what happened that brought life to an end for so many young men.

But among the many aspects of this valuable exercise, none are of more worth surely, than the opportunity which is offered to survivors and to the families and friends of the casualties, to record their experiences for themselves. When he conducted the memorial service, the Reverend Sandy Young of Ardrossan talked of the importance of the story being told. This helps all of us.

This chapter includes some shipmates telling the story. The following chapter, and very much the last word, includes the stories of the bereaved Their telling, even after the passage of more than fifty years, is the most fitting reason of all for this memorial volume.

# Petty Officer Brian A Philpott

I joined *Dasher* as an aircrew member of 837 Squadron, on 22 January 1943 while she was tied up in Liverpool. I had no regrets when I left her in Scapa Flow five weeks later. My emotions were of considerable relief as we had not achieved any of our objectives.

She had a reputation as a problem ship, which we learned about from other aircrew who had been aboard since she was first commissioned in 1942. These problems related to engine and steering malfunctions. So we were not surprised when they continued in one form or another, during our brief period aboard her. From the air she looked placid enough, but this belied her hidden temperament.

The voyage from Liverpool through the Minches to Scapa Flow was rough and Scapa was wild and desolate. After a few days we were ordered to sail with an escort of three small corvettes towards the island. During the voyage winds of hurricane force struck our portside and flying was out of the question.

The storm force winds were lethal, both to the ship and to the aircraft. Lifeboats and Carley floats were slowly but systematically whipped from their davits and stowage positions and reduced to total wrecks. Speed was maintained and the ship's motion was so chaotic that most of the crew, in particular aircrew, speculated that she was heading for certain capsize.

All hands were called to the flight deck on our second night at sea for the purpose of securing the wires lashing three aircraft to the deck. The ship's pitching and rolling, coupled with the storm force winds had strained the wires to breaking point and since the aircraft had begun to move about it became a matter of urgency to rectify the hazardous situation.

It was well nigh impossible to obtain a foothold on the wet flight deck and decisions were soon made to assist the worst of the wildly moving Swordfish over the side. The order was given to clear the flight deck and we did not need to be told twice, in what was an atrocious situation. The next morning the Swordfish we had left on the flight deck had disappeared, leaving only a few tangled wires and other lashings.

If the flight deck was a hazardous place to be, the hangar was little better, except that it was shielded from the worst of the gale force winds and the driving snow squalls. In exactly the same way that the lashings had worked loose on the flight deck, so they replicated the procedure in the hangar. Aircraft began to tug at their lashings, which further loosened them and allowed Swordfish to career into Swordfish and Hurricane to career into Hurricane with disastrous results.

The problem was then compounded by the loosening of ties and wires securing spare Hurricanes to the hangar roof, which ultimately fell on the aircraft moving around on the hangar floor. To add to this melee, the air fitters' and air mechanics' tool boxes broke loose from their stowage and started sliding from port to starboard and back again. Like the flight deck, the hangar was declared out of bounds as it was a danger to life and limb.

It was finally decided that *Dasher* was a liability rather than an asset and she sailed to Iceland to have the damage assessed and temporary repairs carried out prior to sailing to Dundee via Scapa for permanent repairs.

At Scapa Flow, my squadron was moved ashore to the Royal Naval air station at Hatston in Orkney. By the luck of the draw our place was taken by 816 and 891 Squadrons, most of whom were to perish when the explosion occurred.

# Rev Frank Myers

ex Telegraphist HMS *Dasher*

It was with mixed feelings that my name appeared on the draft list in Chatham Barracks for *Dasher*. *Dasher* was in Brooklyn Navy Yard in New York and we were to be part of the initial commissioning party. Arrival in New York brought us a heat wave and having to cope with kitbags and hammocks still dressed in winter uniform. We were in Brooklyn Navy Barracks which, compared with Chatham, was out of this world, not only in standards but in food. Also because the ship was not ready we had New York before us. All the theatres and concerts were available free, from the Carnegie Hall to the Radio City Music Hall, from the cinemas to the shows featuring such as Tommy Dorsey's band. We almost felt guilty enjoying such unrationed and unrestricted lighting conditions, while Britain was suffering utility hardship and darkness.

The time came for working on the ship. What a change from my previous ship, the *Woolston*, a 1917 destroyer—so cramped but obviously dedicated to a warlike purpose. Here was the original merchant superstructure and bridge and large capacity holds with a flight deck superimposed. She had been laid down as a banana boat, the *Rio de Janeiro*.

The journey to the United Kingdom was uneventful, although there were signs of what was to be our lot. She rolled to great extent. There was a feeling of insecurity, but it was our lot to be on the ship and nothing could change it. An operation to the North African landings brought a satisfaction of doing something worthwhile, but after the landings were consolidated, we were no longer required.

Our next operation was to take part in the Russian convoys. The sea was so rough on our way to Iceland that the *Dasher* was badly damaged. There were not a few who were disturbed by the ship's motion. One kept away from the flight deck for to see its slope made it seem impossible to keep any foothold. One officer spent most of the time on the lee of the ship out on deck for fear that she would capsize.

Because of the damage we were ordered back to Dundee for repair. It was in Dundee that I left the ship. One looks back on the appalling loss of life on *Dasher*. Many of my friends were lost there and the tales which were recounted as I met up with the survivors were horrendous—aviation spirit ignited on the water and some men were burned alive.

One might imagine my mixed feelings as I was eventually drafted whilst in the Pacific to a similar ship. Was it to be the same story again? The answer was soon found for lessons had been learned. The *Striker* was a far more stable ship and had many things that *Dasher* didn't, and indeed was a much happier ship to be on. The feeling was that the first four ships, *Archer*, *Avenger*, *Biter* and *Dasher* were adapted too quickly without much thought behind them. They were nicknamed 'Woolworth Carriers'.

After becoming a minister in Springburn, Glasgow. I conducted two funerals, one soon after the other. One was for a woman who had not got over the death of her favourite nephew in 1943. He left home in the morning and never came back. He was on *Dasher*. Soon after at the second funeral I was introduced to the widow's sister, whose husband was killed on *Dasher*. He was a seaman who did hairdressing on his off-watch time and had many times cut my hair. This experience compelled me to go to Ardrossan to look at the graves of the bodies recovered (so few). One was someone I should have known but didn't and could only come to the conclusion that he was my relief.

One wonders why it took fifty years for the truth to be told. We are only thankful that the truth is now known and that these men who were lost are now remembered.

# Petty Officer Jeff Gray

Jeff swam to the floats which were furthest away to allow his shipmates who were not good swimmers the opportunity to clamber aboard the nearest floats. Whilst in the water he saved two lives.

*Petty Officer Jeff Gray (1939). Inset Jeff Gray (1994)*

CHAPTER 13

# CHERISHED MEMORIES

## Dennis Roberts (aged 20)

Dennis Roberts was born on 22nd January 1923. He had a
brother and a sister, Eric and Ethel. On leaving John Brights
Secondary School, Llandudno at the age of fifteen, he started
work as an apprentice motor mechanic with a local garage. He
was very happy working with vehicles as he enjoyed fixing
anything mechanical. At his home, Pink Farm, Great Orme,
Llandudno, he loved to drive his father's car up and down the
long driveway.

Dennis joined the Merchant Navy. However after a few
voyages back and forth to Canada, he left and went back to the
family farm for a spell. Dennis then rejoined the Merchant
Navy at Liverpool as an ordinary rating and travelled to
Brooklyn to join the ill-fated *Dasher*.

He stayed with the ship for the next seven months and in his
letters to his family he always wrote that *Dasher* was always in
trouble and not really sea-worthy.

Dennis's parents received a telegram stating that their son was Missing Presumed Killed. The date was April 1st 1943 and at first they thought it was a joke.

Dennis's mum and dad, brother Eric and sister Ethel never got over their sad loss. The front door of the family home was never locked in case Dennis should ever turn up. Dennis's last letter was written on board *Dasher* and dated 20th March 1943, one week before the disaster.

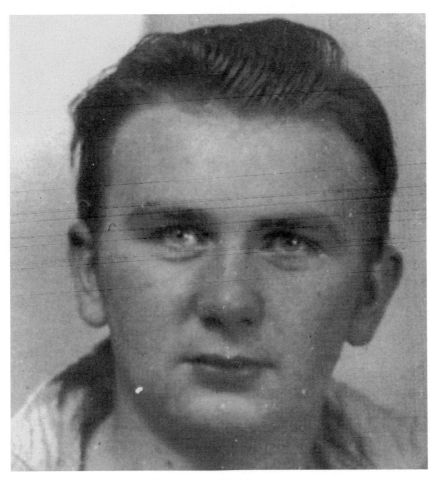

*Dennis Roberts—photo taken on board* Dasher

*Dennis Roberts (third from l) with some shipmates aboard* Dasher

# Mrs Francis Hook, Zimbabwe

Mrs Hook last saw her brother, Norman George Rogerson when he was sixteen years old. He left South Africa and joined the Fleet Air Arm. Four years later he was a flight engineer aboard *Dasher* when the ship blew up and sank.

Norman's family were informed by telegram that he was Lost At Sea. Due to wartime censorship no other details were released. The only information that Mrs Hook had was that her brother was serving on HMS *Dasher*.

In 1993, a relative posted a cutting from an Ayrshire newspaper. It was regarding the first ever church service and dedication ceremony to mark the loss of HMS *Dasher* and many of her crew.

Mrs Francis Hook and her husband John willingly made the long journey from Harare, Zimbabwe, thankful after fifty years finally to be able to pay tribute to her brother and his shipmates.

## Thomas Bretherton
## (aged 19)

Able Seaman/Stoker

Tommy resided at 54 Hartfield Crescent Birmingham. He was the second eldest of nine children and he enjoyed camping, cycling, walking and fishing. He worked as a bread roundsman with a local company.

He wanted to join the services so as he was only seventeen, he asked his dad to sign the forms as he was under age. His dad agreed and in 1941 he joined the navy. In 1942 he joined HMS *Dasher* some of the ratings referred to as 'The Death Tub' due to 'something always going wrong'.

During his last stay at home on leave, he was very quiet and not his usual cheery self. On the day he was due to leave home to rejoin *Dasher*, he said to his brother, 'Look after mum and the kids and you can have my bike.'

He left his flask and packed lunch on the table. He left money on the shelf and he also left clothes that he always took with him in a drawer. Tommy's family believe that he knew this would be his last leave and he would not be returning.

# Thomas John Alexander Moore

Ty Sub Lieutenant (E) RNR

Thomas was born in March 1902 at 189 Allison Street, Govanhill, Glasgow. He attended Govanhill school and then served an apprenticeship as a marine engineer. He joined David McBrayne Ltd, shipping company to the islands of North West Scotland eventually serving as chief engineer on board RMS *Lochinver* in the Outer Hebrides.

Thomas met and married Bella McKenzie whose mother owned and managed Plockton Hotel, West Ross-shire. He gave up the sea and managed the Plockton Hotel with his wife.

In 1939 at the outbreak of war, Thomas went back to sea and he eventually joined HMS *Dasher* with the rank of Sub Lieutenant.

On Friday 26th March 1943 *Dasher* was at anchor in the Clyde. Thomas was granted shore leave on that day and he was due back on board on Saturday 27th March, the next day. He was to board at Greenock on the Saturday evening.

He visited his brother in Glasgow on the Friday and as he did not have time to visit his wife in Plockton with his two daughters and newborn son (whom he had never seen) he decided just to return to his ship early. He took the train from Glasgow to Ardrossan and from there he sailed by Liberty boat to board *Dasher*. Once aboard he arranged for his relief to go ashore that night. His relief was pleased to have the chance to receive one extra day and night ashore.

As a result of Thomas going back aboard a day early, he went down with his ship.

*(see picture p184)*

*Survivors Eddie Cane & Eric Hayward*
*After giving his evidence for the text of this book, Eddie died on 22 March*
*1995*

# Thomas Harrop (aged 21)

Air Fitter (E) Fleet Air Arm

Thomas lived at Crabmill Lane Coventry with his father, Lewis and his mother, Mary, five sisters and two brothers. He had a very happy childhood and enjoyed sport, especially cricket. He attended Broad Street school and was particularly keen on woodwork. When he was old enough he joined the Boys Brigade.

Thomas was born in the country village of Goxhill, near Coventry, As he grew older, his friends called him Happy, because he always had a smile on his face.

As an apprentice tool maker his job ensured that he was exempt from war service. However he applied for special release and joined the Fleet Air Arm. On his last leave he was reluctant to rejoin *Dasher* as he was of the opinion that it was an unlucky ship. Thomas did rejoin his ship which was anchored in the Clyde and two days later his parents received that dreadful telegram. They thought there must have been a mistake. However the Admiralty confirmed that Thomas was Missing Presumed Killed. His parents died without ever knowing what had happened to their son.

No photographs of Thomas survive because of the blitz on Coventry when the family home was destroyed.

## Ronald Alan Farthing (aged 20)

Assistant Cook

Ronald was born on the 31st October 1922 and lived with his parents, George and Lillian at 11 Leyes Road, Custom House, London E16. He went to Shipman Road school where he was the goalkeeper for the school football team.

When he left school he was employed as a driver's mate. Ronald joined the merchant navy because a friend of his had joined at the beginning of the war and was reported to be having a wonderful time. On completion of his training Ronald travelled to America in 1942 for the commissioning of *Dasher*. He joined as a scullion and was later promoted to assistant cook. He was on board on disaster day and was lost with hundreds of his shipmates.

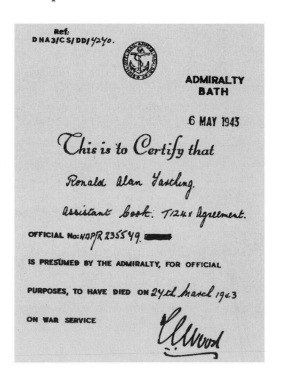

*Assistant Cook Ronald Alan Farthing*
*(Opposite) Admiralty death certificate*

# John Lyle McFarlane

Sub Lieutenant

John was a native of Greenock. He enjoyed sports and had taken part in the Scottish Football League. He had also won a number of medals at his golf club.

John was an electrician with Greenock Corporation and an officer in the 2nd Greenock Boys Brigade. He enjoyed singing at functions and loved life.

He celebrated his twenty first birthday on 24th March a few days before the disastrous 27th March 1943. John's sister and his mother live in Newcastle.

*John Lyle McFarlane—buried in Greenock*

# George S Anderson (aged 22)

Air Mechanic Fleet Air Arm

George was born in Philipstoun, a village three miles east of Linlithgow. His mother and father, Grace and George, had two other sons, James and William. George attended Linlithgow Academy and played football in the local team. He enjoyed a game of tennis.

Known as the life and soul of the party, he enjoyed life to the full as much as he enjoyed being a member of the Boys Brigade. When he left school he got a job as mechanic with Ransom Engineering, Corstorphine, Edinburgh.

In 1940 he was called up for navy service and went to Gosforth for training, on completion of which he was transferred to HMS *Jackdaw* in Crail, Fife, then to Machrihanish in the Mull of Kintyre. From there, George joined *Dasher*. George's name, along with others lost during the war, is inscribed on a plaque in St Michael's Church, Linlithgow.

*George Anderson, Air Mechanic*

## Percy Charles Hodkinson (aged 24)

Telegraphist

Percy was born on June 1st 1918. This date was his parents' fourth wedding anniversary. His mother was deaf and dumb; his father deaf but with speech. On leaving school at the age of fifteen, he worked as a clerk with Ribble Motors bus company in Preston, his home town.

Shortly after his twenty first birthday, he went to Manchester to train with the Deaf Association as a welfare officer for the deaf. In 1941 he entered service with the Royal Navy and later that year he married Ann. In September 1942, his son David was born. Percy was able to come home on a few occasions. He was on home leave in February 1943, one month before the tragic event.

A wife with a young son, a mother, a father and a sister were left to mourn his death, the manner of which was unknown to them until fifty years later in 1993.

The Deaf Association *Quarterly News* announced the death of Percy with an obituary and photograph.

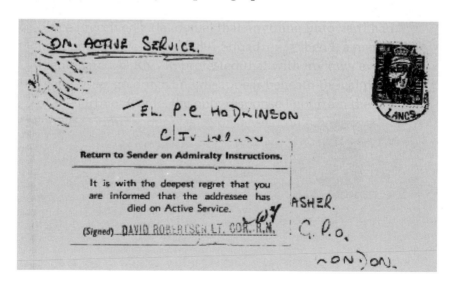

*(above) Percy Charles Hodkinson, Telegraphist*
*(opposite) Percy Hodkinson's sister wrote him a letter on the day of the disaster . . . the envelope was returned with a sticker message*

## Cecil John Davis (aged 21)

Ordinary Telegraphist

Cecil was a shipmate of John Melville. This photograph of Cecil came from John Melville's family. John and Cecil were buried in the same lair at Ardrossan cemetery.

*Cecil John Davis, Ordinary Telegraphist*

## Richard (Dickie) Liddle (aged 27)

Ordinary Seaman

Dickie was six feet tall. He had a fresh complexion and dark curly hair. His first job was as a bus conductor. His second job was in furniture sales and then he decided to further his career by joining the police force. His station was in Gosforth, Northumbria.

Dickie had two sisters, Francis and Bella. At Bella's wedding reception, Dickie stood up and gave an excellent rendition of *Westering Home* which was greatly appreciated by all the guests. Not only was he an accomplished singer, he also enjoyed playing the violin.

His mother and father never ever got over the sudden and very sad loss of their loveable son. In April 1943, a relative of Dickie, Mrs Betty Johnstone who lives in Beith, Ayrshire was visiting Stevenston. As she walked arm in arm with her husband on the beach, they came across a large number of sailors' hats floating in the water. Mrs Johnstone was at that time unaware of the tragic event which had taken place.

## William E Clark (aged 21)

Leading Seaman

Bill was shy but likeable. He was one of a large famiily comprising nine boys and three girls. He attended Cockernhoe Church of England school on the outskirts of Luton. On leaving school he worked in a bakery ship and when he was 17 he volunteered for the Royal Navy. He was based at Chatham before joining *Warsprite*. In 1942 he travelled to New York to join *Dasher* and he remained with the ship during its seven month career.

## Richard (Surname Unknown)

*Richard (surname unknown)*
*a shipmate of John Melville (October 1941)*

# William (Bill) Candlish (aged 34)

Bill was born at Platt Run, Crosshouse at 11.45pm on 3rd October 1909. His mum, Jane and his dad, Henry had four of a family, Bill, Colin, Mary and Carrie.

Bill married Agnes (Nan) Young at the Cooperative Hall, Crosshouse on 18th November 1932 and they had a family comprising Harry (born 1933), Nancy (born 1938) and Janette (born 1940).

In civilian life Bill was a fire clay sink maker. Prior to and after joining the Royal Navy, Bill answered to the nickname of Skid.

*Bill Candlish on leave with family*

*John Melville, Ordinary Coder*

# John Melville (aged 37)

Ordinary Coder

John was a native of Dunfermline and worked for the British Linen Bank in the town. He was a noted baritone singer and enjoyed singing in the Dunfermline Abbey choir and the Edinburgh Grand Opera choir.

He worked for the bank in Newcastleton, Newton St Boswells and Haddington before being transferred to Galashiels where he and his wife spent five happy years. During this time John was a member of the East Church choir and the Galashiels Amateur Operatic Society.

John served as a group warden in the Civil Defence in Galashiels prior to volunteering for the Royal Navy. He was serving aboard *Dasher* as a coder on that fateful day.

His body was brought ashore at Ardrossan and on Wednesday 31st March 1943 John was buried with full naval honours in the local cemetery. His marriage was blessed with the birth of a daughter, Isobel, who was three years old when her father died.

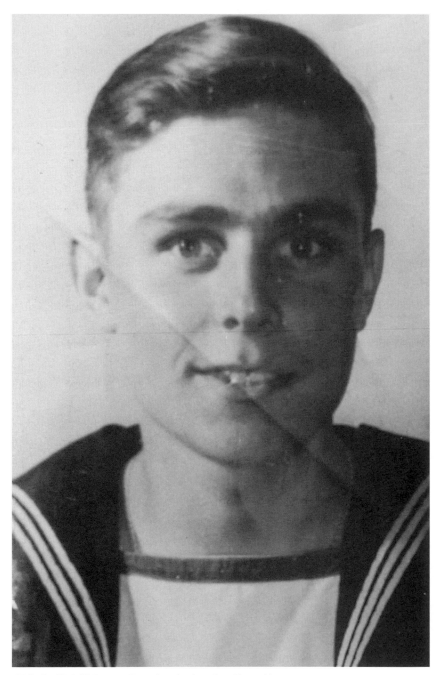

*Edwin (Dick) James Dando, Acting Leading Airman*

# Edwin (Dick) James Dando (aged 22)

Acting Leading Airman

Dick and I knew each other before the war as young teenagers when I was 14 and he was 16. He had lovely blue eyes and blond hair and he had started work in a shipping company. We both lived in London but I was evacuated to Huntingdon and Dick's firm moved to Watford.

We started corresponding and when I left school I lived with an aunt in Nottingham. When the bombing was at its height in London I learned from Dick that he was joining the Fleet Air Arm and he was sent to Worthy Down, Winchester. He qualified as a Wireless Operator/Air Gunner which was not easy, as he suffered from air sickness. To control the urge to be sick, he would grip a pencil in his teeth.

Dick visited me in Nottingham and encouraged me to move back to London since he had weekend leaves from Worthy Down. I transferred to the Ministry of Health in Whitehall but three weeks later Dick was transferred to Machrihanish.

When he was allowed leave we had great times together and by this time we had met each other's family. Though we were so young he talked about the future we might have together. On his last leave, we went to the theatre to see *Dancing Years* by Ivor Novello.

After Dick returned to duty, I was in the office typing and my supervisor told me that I was wanted on the telephone. It was a terrible shock to be informed that Dick was missing.

Everything was kept very hush-hush and we imagined that his plane had crashed into the sea and he had come to grief. From age 14 to age 16, Dick was the love of my life and I reflect how lucky I was to have known such a sweet and good humoured person who was always tender and caring.

Mrs Christine Joblin (nee Smith)

# William MacDonald

Air Mechanic

On arrival at HMS *Fortitude* (Ardrossan Harbour) William was taken by ambulance to the Royal Navy Sick Quarters (8 South Beach Road, Ardrossan).

William was so badly burned, it was deemed wise not to convey him to Ballochmyle Hospital. While he received the best of treatment from the Royal Navy doctors and medical staff at Ardrossan, on day thirteen he passed away. He was buried in Ardrossan Cemetery with full naval honours on 12th April 1943.

*Dasher*'s motor launch MV *528*, which had been on duty during deck landing practice had moved in immediately to pick up survivors. The crew of MV *528* were astonished to see a man in the water holding onto a kitbag. He was about four hundred yards from *Dasher*.

When they lifted him out of the water, William was almost unconscious. His face and chest were badly burnt and the skin had been blasted off his hands. In the Sick Bay at Ardrossan, William told how he had been taking his shaving gear out of his kitbag when he heard the explosion, but after that he knew nothing until he woke up in ML *528*.

At that time William was the sole survivor of the blast which destroyed the Fleet Air Arm messdeck. Incredibly he had been blown some four hundred yards through the hole in *Dasher*'s side.

# Leslie L Falla

Ordinary Telegraphist

Leslie could not swim. He jumped over the side of the ship and made it to a Carley float. He was on the float when the sea burst into flames. Leslie was engulfed. His crew mates could do nothing for him owing to the intense heat and the speed of the flames on the surface of the sea.

# Thomas H Neighbour (aged 21)

Able Seaman

Thomas was born on Christmas Day 1922. He had four brothers, Joseph, Francis, Terry and William. He also had a sister who had the same name as his mum, Catherine Emma. His dad's name was also Thomas.

Thomas attended Foster Road School, Islington, North London. He was always the family favourite and he enjoyed football and dancing, although his sister always suspected that he only went to the dancing to look after her.

Thomas never ever spoke about *Dasher* and on his last leave his sister asked him not to go back, but he would not hear of it.

When Thomas perished, he left behind a sorely grieving family and a loving sweetheart, Masie Freeman. Thomas's mother never ever looked forward to Christmas after the tragedy as her son had been born on Christmas Day.

*Angus Cameron on leave with his parents and sister Irene*

## Sub Lieutenant Angus Cameron (aged 24)

Angus was born in Edinburgh on 2nd October 1918. He stayed there with his parents William and Ina and his sister Irene. Twelve years later the family moved to Glasgow and Angus was educated at Allan Glen's school.

Although Angus's parents wished him to become a chemist, his chosen career was in engineering and on reaching school leaving age, he was apprenticed to Rowan and Company, Glasgow. After his apprenticeship, Angus joined the Clan Line and served aboard the *Stirlingshire*.

Angus was a single man and he was engaged to be married to a girl in America. When on leave he was kept busy with his many hobbies which included cycling, fishing, swimming and rugby. On many occasions he cycled from Glasgow to Ardrossan to visit one of his friends, Jim Martin who worked for the newspaper in Ardrossan.

Irene's birthday was on 22nd March and in the third week in March 1943 Angus telephoned home to wish his sister a very happy birthday. During the conversation Angus said, Tell mum to sleep tonight.

These five words were in fact a family code which meant that his ship was in home waters. The family never recovered from their very sad loss. Six months after they received the dreaded telegram, Angus's mother died.

## Petty Officer John G Stamp

John was a tall well-built man with sandy coloured hair and blue eyes. He was the eldest son of caring loving parents, Annie and John. His three brothers were George, Harry and Alfred, his two sisters were Vera and Ann.

John was born and bred in South Shields where he attended Laygate Lane Baptist Church. He joined their Boys Brigade Company and became an officer.

He became involved with Royal Navy Volunteer Reserve at their base HMS *Satellite*. To John, being a member of the RNVR became more than just a hobby.

Before the start of the Second World War, John was a crew member on coal ships that plied their trade from the River Tyne. John later served on a minesweeper, then on the Russian run on HMS *Curlew*, before joining *Dasher*.

John was Dasher's Executive Officer, Lt Commnader Lane's right hand man. His Commander thought very highly of John. As a son and brother, John was truly loved and respected. He was classed as an honest gentleman who was always willing to help anyone in need. He is sorely missed by all his family.

John's brother George was lost at sea four months before the *Dasher* tragedy whilst serving aboard *Wydestone*.

*Petty Officer John G Stamp*

*George Wood (on right)*

*Thomas Moore (see story p161)*

# George Wood

Fireman

George was born on 24th September 1905 in Ellon Aberdeenshire. He was the third son of a family of four boys and three girls. The parents were Alex and Mary.

The family moved to Bridge of Weir when George was four years old. He went to Killalan Primary school and then to Bridge of Weir Secondary school. He left school at age fourteen to begin his apprenticeship as a baker. His hobbies were football and dancing. He was a member of the Young Men's Guild at Freeland Church and played in their football team that won the Scottish Churches League in 1934/35.

George continued working as a baker until, in 1939, he and four other local lads volunteered for the Merchant Navy. 1939 was also the year he married Betty McCauley from Tollcross Glasgow.

His first ship was the *Salopian* which was torpedoed in 1941. His next ship the *Karanga*, a troop ship, was hit and sunk by enemy action. George survived this sinking as well and in 1942 he was transferred to *Dasher*.

In late March 1943 George was on shore leave, visiting his pregnant wife and his daughter. On his last day of leave, he left home very early in the morning and made his way to Greenock to board the first pilot boat which took him out to *Dasher*. The date was 27th March 1943, disaster day.

## William Clark

William was lost when the *Dasher* disaster occurred and the family never ever found out what had happened as no details were forthcoming from the Admiralty.

In 1986 his brother John wrote to the *Sunday Post* appealing for information surrounding the sinking. As a result of the publication of their letter, John and his wife Margaret were deluged with over two hundred replies. They had opened up the floodgates which had kept survivors and relatives apart.

Officers and men who had survived the tragedy, mothers, fathers, brothers, sisters and cousins, all wrote to John and Margaret who were now in a position to piece together some of the details regarding the loss of ship.

John and Margaret were of immense help to survivors and bereaved relatives. They managed to assist survivors to renew old friendships and for bereaved relatives to correspond with long lost friends.

---

### *Did you know my father?*

# GEORGE ARTHUR (JIMMY) HABGOOD

### Ship's Butcher on HMS Dasher; drowned.

My father, G A Habgood, died when I was a baby, and I know very little about him.
Do you remember him? Could you tell me anything about him - what he looked like, what kind of person he was, anything he said to you.
If so, I would be very grateful if you would contact me.
Telephone 0689 870344 (reversing the charges),
or write to Judith Everett, 5 Woodhurst Avenue, Petts Wood, Orpington, Kent BR5 1AR

---

*Bill Clark*

# The announcement of the loss

With the ending of hostilities, the Admiralty had no reason to withhold information on the loss of ships. Where it was believed the enemy were not in possession of the facts, losses had not been published. Among other losses announced in May 1945 was the sinking of HMS *Dasher* more than two years previously. The following cuttings from the *Daily Record* and the *Scottish Daily Express* brought news of Dasher's fate to the public for the first time.

# Carrier Sunk By Own Plane

FROM OUR OWN CORRESPONDENT

BEHIND the announcement by the Admiralty that the escort-carrier Dasher was sunk on March 27, 1943, lies the story of the most appalling naval tragedy in the history of the Clyde

It was a dull, hazy Saturday afternoon when watchers on the Ayrshire and Arran coasts saw a sheet of flame leap from the Dasher, then steaming slowly in the main channel, and heard a dull explosion which shattered windows several miles away.

A few minutes later they saw the ship stand on, its stern " and rapidly disappear.

Nothing was published of the tragedy at the time, all stories being stopped by the censor, who allowed no details to pass.

The Dasher, a U.S. merchantman which had been converted into an escort-carrier, and was at the time being used as a Fleet Air Arm training ship, was concluding operations for the day.

On board some hundreds of liberty men were making ready to go ashore. Few reached land alive.

**The cause of the disaster has never been officially made known, but it is believed that one of the Dasher's planes coming in to land misjudged the situation and crashed into a store of oil drums and explosives.**

## INFERNO OF FLAMES

There was a tremendous shattering roar, and almost immediately the ship was enveloped in an inferno of flames. A minute or two later her bows reared up almost perpendicularly, and she quickly slipped under in a cloud of smoke and steam.

Then followed the most tragic part of all A number of her crew had jumped overboard or had been hurled into the water by the explosion. Suddenly from the sunken ship a great spout of oil gushed to the surface

Craft of all kinds which had hastened to the rescue both from Arran and from Ayrshire ports were driven back, and were for some hours heavily hampered in their rescue efforts by flames and smoke.

Meanwhile, on shore at Ardrossan, an S O S had been sent out. Later in the evening a number of rescued men were landed, and at once rushed to hospital.

Those who had escaped injury or burning were taken to hurriedly-prepared billets. Other survivors landed in Arran were removed to the Arran Cottage Hospital at Lamlash. No casualty figures have ever been issued, but it is believed that more than 400 men were lost from a crew of some six hundred.

## ESCORT CARRIER LOST

### War Disaster Recalled— Burials at Ardrossan

Now that the war against Germany has come to an end, it is possible to make reference to a serious naval disaster which took place near Ardrossan on 27th March, 1943. The escort carrier "Dasher," whose loss is now announced by the Admiralty, was sunk in the Firth of Clyde between Arran and North Ayrshire as a result of an internal explosion. No official announcement has been issued regarding the number of lives lost but it is unofficially stated that over 400 perished.

Local people who were in the vicinity of the harbour at the time state that the vessel seemed suddenly to blaze up and then sink very rapidly. The noise of the explosion was heard over a considerable area, and for a time speculation was rife as to its cause. All available ships immediately went out to pick up survivors, but blazing oil on the water hampered their efforts.

In Ardrossan urgent calls were sent out for doctors, ambulance drivers and stretcher-bearers, and some members of the voluntary wartime services received the call when attending one or other of the local cinemas. The wounded brought into Ardrossan were conveyed to hospital, and other rescued officers and men were found billets in the town. The ladies of the Church of Scotland Canteen, Ardrossan, gave much appreciated assistance in providing tea and biscuits to the rescued men and the ladies of the local W.V.S. also gave valuable help, furnishing from the stock at their premises clothes for the men. Many sad sights were witnessed, but the survivors showed a great spirit of cheerfulness and courage.

The bodies of fourteen members of the crew were brought to Ardrossan and taken to the A.R.P. mortuary at the top of Glasgow Street. Two were buried in their own home towns and the remaining twelve in Ardrossan Cemetery. The gallant dead were accorded full naval honours. The coffins, each covered with the Union Jack, rested on a motor lorry, and immediately behind motor cars were provided for the relatives of the deceased. The procession included a firing party and a naval band as well as a large representation of the Royal Navy and W.R.N.S. As the procession, at the head of which marched Capt. J. L. Field, R.N. slowly wended its way up Glasgow Street and along Parkhouse Road, its passing was watched in respectful silence by large crowds of spectators. This was undoubtedly the largest funeral procession ever seen in Ardrossan.

One of the injured died a few days later in the Naval Hospital and he also was buried at Ardrossan Cemetery with naval honours. Two bodies of members of the crew that were washed ashore were interred at Ayr.

The graves of these thirteen men in Ardrossan cemetery are well tended by Mr Gardiner and his staff, and flowers are also regularly supplied by ladies of the local W.V.S. and by friends of the deceased.

*CLYDE SECRET CAN BE TOLD*

# Crowds see carrier blow up

Express Staff Reporter

IN the full light of the afternoon of March 27, 1943, the escort carrier Dasher sailed up the Firth of Clyde, reared up on end after an internal explosion poised for a few minutes

with her flight deck almost vertical, then plunged to the bottom, stern first.

Nearly 500 of her crew of 600 were lost within sight of hundreds of people in Arran.

Dasher, a converted U.S. merchantman of medium tonnage, was used as a Fleet Air Arm training ship.

A few minutes before planes had been taking off and landing on her flight deck.

Her liberty men, in their "No. 1 suits," were ready to go ashore when she berthed in 15 minutes.

Cause of the disaster—the most serious in Clyde history—is not definitely known.

The roar of the explosion brought people rushing out of their houses in Brodick, Ardrossan, Saltcoats, Irvine, Troon, and Largs, and shattered hundreds of window-panes.

## TO RESCUE

More than 20 ships — from destroyers to small coasters—sped towards the stricken carrier.

Eight miles away a man was watching through a powerful telescope.

"I could not believe my eyes," he said. "It seemed only a moment since I had seen the explosion, and now the sea was empty, with rescue ships dashing towards the spot from all directions."

Within seconds of Dasher's disappearance, a pool of oil and petrol shot to the surface and caught fire. The surface of the sea blazed fiercely over a wide area. Dense masses of heavy black smoke drifted across the firth.

It was impossible for would-be rescuers to get close to pick up

# Carrier blew up in Clyde

**◼ CONTINUED ◼**

survivors. Barely a hundred swam to safety through the inferno of smoke and flame.

Doctors, ambulance men, and all available cars were rushed to the waterfront after notices had been flashed on local cinema screens appealing for help.

Eighty survivors were brought to the mainland, those less seriously injured being taken in by householders until they could be removed to hospital.

An Ardrossan woman described the explosion as the most deafening noise, imaginable."

"I ran to the window and saw huge clouds of dense black smoke blowing in towards the coast." she added.

James Holmes (19) said that flames gushed out of the ship. They coloured the sky, even though it was still clear daylight. "The blast cracked both our front windows."

## CLEARLY SEEN

The aircraft carrier's last moments were seen clearly from Arran, as a fairly strong breeze was blowing the smoke in the opposite direction towards the mainland.

William McAuslin, of the Royal Observer Corps. Brodick, who saw it through binoculars from a hut 300ft. up in the Arran hills, telephoned the authorities the moment he saw smoke belch out of the carrier's stern and sides.

"I had been watching a couple of Swordfish planes practising landings on her flight deck. After sailing quite close inshore she changed course towards the mainland and was stern on to me when I noticed a huge burst of smoke.

"It subsided a moment later, and a friend who was with me said: 'Do you think she's all right?'

"The carrier seemed to be on an even keel, but suddenly I said, 'Oh heavens, she's going!' A moment later she sank like a stone. The whole thing—from the explosion to her final disappearance—took only five minutes.

## THREE RAFTS

"I still had my glasses trained on the spot. Immediately afterwards I could only see what looked like three rafts on the surface. I counted seven or eight people on one, not so many on the second, and there seemed to be only one on the third.

"A minute or two later the whole sea seemed to be on fire."

Mr. H. P. McWalter, a Brodick hotel keeper and an ex-Merchant Navy man, said: "She went down so quickly that it seemed as if the ship's bottom must have been blown out. Just after the explosion I saw her take a heavy list to starboard. One of her planes slid down the steeply-listing deck and fell into the sea.

"The ship seemed to stand on end while I counted three, then she slid under."

# The Wreck of HMS Dasher

Surveys carried out by the Wrecks Section, Hydrographic Office, Ministry of Defence

| | |
|---|---|
| 12th January 1944 | Wreck located 553800 North, 045700 West. Five miles south of Little Cumbrae island |
| 8th May 1956 | Position as above |
| 17th January 1969 | Large wreck located in steep slope at above position |
| 25th February 1976 | Not detected by dual channel side scan (DCS3). No close search of position taken |
| 23rd January 1981 | Wreck located, reported to be 'possibly Dasher' |
| 16th April 1982 | Wreck positively identified as Dasher lies upright in 170 metres; flight deck intact at 140 metres; located by naval party 1007 |
| 17th April 1984 | Dasher located and side scan sonar image taken; survey carried out by HMS Beagle |
| 13th May 1985 | Result of survey shows Dasher upright, lying east/west with raised bridge towards west end; several small contacts located around Dasher. |

The above small contacts would appear to be:

1 the lone Hurricane which slithered off the flight deck into the water, seconds prior to the ship sinking. When this aircraft hit the water, it went straight under without floating;

2 ship's fitments which had worked loose as the aircraft carrier sank to the bottom of the Clyde estuary.

Note: the position of the wreck is almost exactly halfway on the ferry journey between Brodick and Ardrossan.

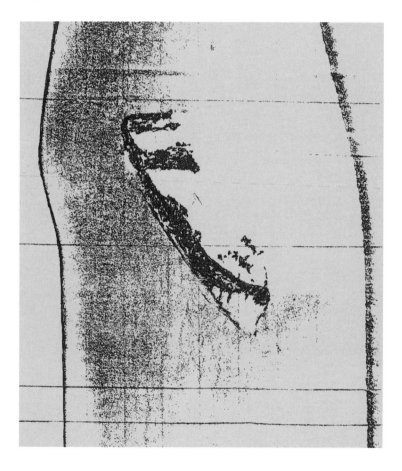

*©Crown Copyright 1995 published by permissison of the Controller of Her Majesty's Stationery Office. Reproduced from a Side-Scan Sonar Image of HMS* Dasher *taken by HMS* Beagle *in 1984*